napa bulletin 7

T0340788

Applied Anthropologist and Public Servant: The Life and Work of Philleo Nash

■ Ruth H. Landman and
Katherine Spencer Halpern, eds.

National Association for the Practice of Anthropology
A Unit of the American Anthropological Association

NAPA Bulletins are occasional publications of the National Association for the Practice of Anthropology, a Unit of the American Anthropological Association.

Ralph J. Bishop and Pamela Amoss
General Editors

Library of Congress Cataloging-in-Publication Data

Applied anthropologist and public servant.

(NAPA bulletin ; 7)
Bibliography: p.
1. Nash, Philleo, 1909–1987. 2. Anthropologists
—United States—Biography. 3. Applied anthropol-
ogy—United States. I. Landman, Ruth H. II.
Halpern, Katherine Spencer. III. Nash, Philleo,
1909–1987. IV. Series.
GN21.N38A85 1989 306′.092′4 83-34441
ISBN 0-913167-28-0 (pbk.)

ISBN 0-913167-28-0

Contents

Philleo Nash, 1909–1987

Preface

Ruth H. Landman and Katherine Spencer Halpern

With this collection of reminiscences, the National Association for the Practice of Anthropology joins forces with the Society for Applied Anthropology to celebrate one of our most venturesome colleagues. Philleo Nash's anthropological education began at the University of Wisconsin and continued at the University of Chicago in the early 1930s. By 1941 he was drawn into wartime activities. This marked the beginning of a series of applied roles that were more wide-ranging than those of any other anthropologist to date.

Like many anthropologists of his era, Philleo worked as a government anthropologist during the Second World War, based in the Office of War Information. Unlike most of his colleagues, however, he stayed on after the war to become, first, a special assistant in the White House, and then, at the end of President Truman's term, an administrative assistant to the president (McNett 1988). Certainly unique among his anthropological peers, he then ran successfully for statewide political office in his home state of Wisconsin, where he served as Lieutenant Governor, and then as Chair of the Democratic Party. When John F. Kennedy was elected to the presidency, Philleo returned to the federal government as Commissioner of Indian Affairs, a post that he retained for some years in the Johnson administration. Thus it is probably safe to say that he has held both the highest U.S. elective and appointive offices achieved by any member of our profession.

His ties to Wisconsin also led to continued involvement in private business. He assumed the presidency of a family enterprise, the Biron Cranberry Company, Inc., and eventually, during a subsequent return to Wisconsin, became its manager as well. Today, a good many anthropologists have followed Philleo into yet another kind of private enterprise—consulting firms; he was engaged in consulting beginning in the mid-1960s, working especially with the Phillips Petroleum Company, which was headed by William Keeler, an Oklahoma Cherokee who was then the principal tribal chief.

When you look at the reports, speeches, papers, and congressional testimony that Philleo Nash lists in a c.v. he prepared about a year before he died, it is clear that he remained active as an anthropologist. He continued to publish articles based on research in American Indian communities, and he continued to be active in professional societies. He was president of the Society for Applied Anthropology, president of the Anthropological Society of Washington, Secretary to Section H (Anthropology) of the American Association for the Advancement of Science, and treasurer of the American Anthropological Association. No wonder that both the AAA and the SfAA singled him out for awards: the SfAA honored him with its Bronislaw Malinowski Award and the AAA with its Distinguished Service Award. Among his achievements we must count the acclamation of his peers.

But we are still not done: Philleo Nash also rose to the top in education. He was president for many years of the Georgetown Day School in Washington, where his active participation abundantly demonstrated his lifelong commitment to learning and teaching. At the beginning and conclusion of his professional career he held full-time university teaching appointments—from 1937 to 1940 at the University of Toronto, and from 1971 to his retirement as Professor Emeritus in 1977, at the American University in Washington.

Certain threads run through all these activities: there was the lifelong goal of racial equality, which Philleo pursued in many ways. He helped to found Georgetown Day as an integrated school because at the time Washington was a segregated city. Blacks and other minorities were denied rights in the army and in the government generally, and it was in this area that much of Philleo's work during the war, and subsequently on Truman's staff, was concentrated. (See Appendix 1 for some information on source materials for this period.) He felt that his approach to civil rights had empirical and theoretical bases in his early anthropological fieldwork on the Klamath Reservation, where he studied the relationship of religious revival movements to the Indian experience of economic and cultural deprivation following American conquest (1986a:190). His activities in support of justice and equal rights for American Indians were pursued over a long life, but they culminated in his final government position as Commissioner of Indian Affairs.

Anthropological training and fieldwork laid the foundation for Philleo's successes in these bureaucratic and political settings. They help to explain why he succeeded, but in addition, he was willing to be brave—to be heard on behalf of his beliefs. From the safe distance of the years, we can honor him for having drawn Senator Joe McCarthy's enmity as a result of acting on these beliefs while a public servant. At the time, this enmity forced Philleo to reshape his career; thanks to a resiliency and perhaps a basic optimism, he was able to overcome the onus and to see his views become the ascendant morality of the nation.

We think that it is peculiarly fitting that this publication originates in both national associations of practitioner anthropologists. Philleo Nash, we feel sure, would have been delighted by this convergence. But we also think that if he could speak to us today, he would urge us to be more engaged in the public arena, and to follow some of the paths that led to his ability to affect major events.

Note

Acknowledgments. Grateful acknowledgment is made to the College of Arts and Sciences of the American University for an award from the Mellon Fund for Faculty Research and Development that supported the preparation of the manuscript for publication.

Introduction

Ralph J. Bishop, General Editor, NAPA Bulletin Series

The papers in this volume are edited transcripts of addresses delivered at a symposium on the life and work of Philleo Nash held in April 1988 at the annual meeting of the Society for Applied Anthropology. As such, they contain a wealth of personal reminiscences showing, among other things, the great affection and respect in which Dr. Nash was held.

Most important for present and future practitioners, however, are the insights these reminiscences bring to the highly successful career of a pioneer in the field. These insights apply directly to situations practitioners face today.

The title of this Bulletin describes Philleo Nash as "applied anthropologist and public servant." The "and" here is important, because like many practitioners, Nash, though an anthropologist by training, was recognized by other professional labels: businessman, public official, consultant, and educator.

I see a major theme in this collection: the tension that arises between the practitioner's training and his or her calling. Nash's specialized knowledge of anthropology and understanding of cultural issues clearly stood him in good stead as an originator and implementer of public policy, but as he himself said, what he did in these capacities he did in the name of policy, not of anthropology (see page 6 of this volume). Yet when asked to identify his occupation for a biographical reference publication, he listed himself as an "applied anthropologist."

This tension, which most practitioners feel keenly at one time or another, arises from the fact that anthropology takes as its purview everything relating to the human condition. Moreover, traditional graduate education in anthropology requires students to have a broad general knowledge of the field as a whole, as well as deeply specialized knowledge of a much narrower sector. Anthropological training therefore is knowledge-based, not skill-based, even though considerable specific skills are needed to acquire the necessary knowledge.

Since that knowledge is often far more specialized than most full-time non-academic positions require, traditionally trained persons wishing to become practitioners must usually seek employment in positions where the skills they have learned may be applied. The simultaneous breadth and narrowness of anthropology preclude the possibility that many such positions will carry job descriptions headed by the word *anthropologist*.

Practitioners finding themselves in such a situation can learn much from the ways Nash found to resolve it. Throughout this Bulletin, the importance of striking and maintaining a balance emerges over and over again—balance between the role of advocate and the role of administrator, balance between opposing or conflicting approaches to solving a common problem, balance between competing factions or competing demands on one's own time.

Another dominant theme is that of politics. Nash was a successful politician who served in high offices, both appointive and elective. But it becomes clear from reading these pieces that political skills are just as necessary in other careers as they are in public service. In fact, some of the more insightful observations on the political component of work can be found in Edith Rosenfels Nash's account of the Georgetown Day School.

Several contributors, most notably Nancy Lurie, contrast the cultural sensitivity of Nash's approach with the cut-and-dried, by-the-book approach that is most prominently associated in the public mind with bureaucratic organizations. Again the point to remember here is that whatever success Nash had in making his approach stick depended as much on his political savvy as on his anthropological skills.

Although most of Nash's career was spent outside the academic world, he began and ended it as a teacher. Again, this is an important model. The input of successful and innovative practitioners to the training of their successors is essential to the survival and growth of any profession or applied discipline. But even outside academia, Nash was a teacher. All who worked with him report that they learned much from him. Indeed it is a key function of an administrator or manager to help staff members (and clients) develop their skills and knowledge, to act as much the enabler as the supervisor or problem solver.

In Philleo Nash we see a combination of abilities and personal characteristics central to a practitioner's success. Among the abilities: ability to understand a situation's politics, to seek out information and communicate effectively, to balance conflicts, and to understand when, why, and how to act or not on an issue. Among the personal characteristics: openness to people and ideas, commitment to principle, loyalty to friends and supporters, stamina, drive, and optimism.

Anthropologist in the White House

Philleo Nash

Like many other anthropologists of my generation, I came to my first applied job in Washington, D.C., during World War II. I liked the place and the work, never missed the academy, and stayed on after the war—filled with a sense of tasks unfinished. The Truman era turned me on and the McCarthy era did not permanently sour me, although it switched my opportunities to zero at the end of the Truman administration. I turned then to the academy, but the departments I approached were fearful, or discounted my thirteen years of government service as a void, or both.

I left Washington feeling somewhat unwanted both in and out of the academy and was gratified to gain acceptance in the rough and tumble of practical politics. In seven years I made my way from County Chairman to Lieutenant Governor of Wisconsin. I visited and revisited every corner of my native state, made innumerable friends, and some enemies, and gained enormous respect for the political process. In my last try for reelection, I was defeated, so I returned to Washington for a second round, this time as U.S. Commissioner of Indian Affairs. This was satisfactory but not eternal, and after a brief period as a consultant to some multinational clients, I returned to the academy in an established department of anthropology, from which I am an emeritus professor today.

It has been an active, turbulent, personally satisfying career—all of it outside the academy except at the beginning and the end. But was it anthropology or politics? I thought it was anthropology at the time and said so when I made my autobiographical entry in the Wisconsin Blue Book. "Applied Anthropologist," I called myself. Was I right?

In the early part of World War II, I headed a small section in a division of the Domestic Branch of the Office of War Information. Our task was to develop criteria for the evaluation of racial tensions. After correctly forecasting riots in a number of cities, we were naively astonished to find that there was no civilian agency of government willing to receive our information. My associates and I, brash and young, took the problem directly to the White House. There we found a willing, albeit skeptical, listener in a new administrative assistant to President Roosevelt. Jonathan Daniels, journalist and editor, and son of FDR's first boss in the U.S. Navy, was and is an authentic southern liberal. Daniels listened, and that began an association with him that continued up to FDR's death.

President Truman quite literally inherited me, for he knew nothing of me or my work. I came along, so to speak, with the man who was to be my immediate boss during most of the Truman Administration—David K. Niles.

Niles was as authentic a northern liberal as Daniels was southern. His credentials went back to Sacco and Vanzetti and, even before, to the LaFollete-Wheeler presidential campaign of 1924.

Niles and President Truman quickly developed a relationship of trust and confidence in the most delicate areas of human rights. Policy and politics were both served, for Niles soon became Truman's ombudsman to the liberal establishment.

Tragically, Niles's health failed during the last years of the Truman administration. With the support and guidance of others on the Truman staff, I carried on some of his duties, but there could be no real substitute for him.

Truman's Christmas present to me in the last year of his office was the title "Administrative Assistant to the President." But his last day in office was also mine, for I knew there would be no place for me in the new administration.

When I left, I looked back on ten years during which I had worked on one or more aspects of the following national problems: racial tension; civil rights; conscientious objection; self-determination for the Virgin Islands, Puerto Rico, Territory of the Pacific; American Indian affairs; displaced persons; statehood for Hawaii and Alaska; and technical assistance (Point IV).

To say that I worked on these problems means that I prepared research and program memoranda leading to both executive and legislative action; drafted speeches and correspondence; discussed proposals and complaints with delegations; maintained contact with the executive departments; reviewed budget proposals in assigned areas; prepared draft executive orders; made advance preparation for presidential trips; and carried out many other duties, some humdrum, but others filled with tension and excitement. Thus I wrote dozens of letters thanking creative stitchers for their handiwork gifts to the president, but I was also the first to read the letter of instruction found on the body of the Puerto Rican Nationalist who attempted to storm the Blair House and died in an exchange of gunfire with the Secret Service.

The life of the White House staffer is like that of any member of a large organization. Mostly, one tries to be useful from day to day, in whatever areas of opportunity arise. But in the broader sense no one assigned me to duties in detail, and many of the areas into which I ventured were, at the beginning, self-assigned. Those subject areas were consistent with the accepted content of cultural anthropology.

That I was permitted a lot of initiative does not mean that I was unsupervised. The possibility of embarrassing the president by clumsiness or outright failure was ever-present. Of course, I chafed under restraints, but also came to recognize their usefulness. Sharing responsibility with others was a protection. Group effort enhanced the chance of success as much as it reduced the likelihood of failure.

Viewed anthropologically, the presidency is a belief system based on the premise that the president does everything by himself. As he moves through the day, the president engages in various behaviors appropriate to the multiple roles of his office. President Truman used to refer to them as Commander-in-Chief, Chief Politician, Chief Economist, Chief Legislator, Chief of State, and Chief Executive. Reason tells us that no one human being could act out all these roles unaided. Yet, the presidential mystique requires everyone to act as though he did. Media representatives, who are on hand 24 hours a day, continuously evaluate the president's capacity to know, to think, and to decide. But, unsupported by staff initiative, the president can do little. Hence, the White House staffer must learn to do everything as though it were being done by the president, and with the certain knowledge that it is the president who will be held accountable. Living in, working with, and studying this unique culture was my fieldwork for ten years.

With the end of World War II came the lapse of the War Powers Act, which meant a limitation on presidential power and the disappearance of the rationale for our wartime program. Yet, our research suggested that the return of servicemen from overseas would provide the time and place for a repetition of the postwar riots of World War I.

In late 1945 and 1946, our worst predictions came true. It was time to extend theory and practice one more step. My contribution to the program has been deprivation theory: the precursor of violence is protest and the cause is deprivation. Violence can be controlled, but in a democratic society, even one at war, the focus should be on the deprivation and not on the protest. Still, the postwar violence mounted and seemed to be mainly directed at returning black veterans. The fallout, in the form of national indignation, reached President Truman. He really believed in the slogan he kept on his desk—"The Buck Stops Here"—and he demanded a program.

Congress was obviously not ready to act, and neither were the courts. Civil rights legislation and the watershed court decisions were still years away. Presidential action was required, yet there were limits on presidential power. What to do?

In the files, ready for use if the time should ever seem right, was a proposal going back to the early years of the war—a proposal to create a national commission on race relations. It had been rejected then, because it seemed inadequate to the emergency. Now it was all that was possible. Staff work was begun at once under Niles's direction, and the outcome was the President's Committee on Civil Rights.

The Committee's report, "To Secure These Rights," issued in late 1947, was only a report and took no action in and of itself. But it was the first presidentially based document that dealt directly and across the board with such divisive issues as segregation. Some of its most basic recommendations were not acted upon for 17 years, and others have never been adopted. But it began a dialogue about human rights that was necessary to start the process of change. It was a key element in the campaign of 1948 and in Truman's victory. The issue was dramatized as never before in modern times, and successor presidents were bound to follow the lead.

In President Truman's four years, though, there remained the requirement of direct action where opportunities for the Chief Executive were present and results were possible. Developing staff support for such actions was to keep me hard at work for four more years. It was also to bring me into close personal association and eventual friendship with Truman.

Truman kept in close touch and helped me personally in my work after he left the presidency. He had been out of office six years when I ran, with his approval, for Lieutenant Governor of Wisconsin on a platform that included opposition to federal termination of the Menominee Indian tribe. I served only one term, but before I left office my name as President of Wisconsin Senate was on a joint resolution urging Congress to abandon Menominee termination before it was too late. The Congress regrettably did not heed that advice until many years later.

The position I had taken was consistent with the views of anthropology. Yet, I did not run for office as an anthropologist, and when I was defeated for reelection it was not as an anthropologist that I went down.

In 1961, I was nominated by President Kennedy to be U.S. Commissioner of Indian Affairs, and I was confirmed by the U.S. Senate after a prolonged struggle. The struggle had nothing to do with my being an anthropologist, but involved a revival from Wisconsin of the old McCarthy accusations. I was pleased to beat down the smear, and I did not complain about the time it took. But I have to say to other applied anthropologists that I was confirmed in spite of being an anthropologist, not because of it. The Senate of the United States in those days did not think it wise to have a believer in the worth of indigenous cultures serving as Commissioner of Indian Affairs. The Senators confirmed me because President Kennedy, Secretary of the Interior Stewart Udall, and Senator Hubert H. Humphrey refused to back down in the face of diversionary tactics by the opposition.

I was also aided by strong support from the National Congress of American Indians, assembled in convention at just the right time in Lewiston, Idaho. But did these tribal representatives support me because I was known to them as an anthropologist? Not at all. They supported me because I had a clean record on termination, which was then the hottest single issue in American Indian affairs.

There has been a quantum change since World War II. Segregation is on the defensive, and integration, still far from universal, is the norm to be defended. Minority rights are now more often asserted by minority representatives than by elite advocates. Programs for minority benefits are increasingly self-directed. Termination has been replaced by the idea of restoration. Programs that were once developed by presidential power are directed today by commissions organized under their own statutes.

The anthropological view of social policy—that cultural diversity and respect for cultural differences are a requirement of the good life—has had a big advance since 1942. I am inordinately proud of my part in it, and I am grateful to the political leaders who let me do what I would and could. But it was not done in the name of anthropology. It was done in the name of public policy and forged under conditions of extreme social tension.

It appears that anthropologists are now moving into some of the slots once occupied by lawyers, political scientists, economists, psychologists, and sociologists. We are challenged to succeed where others have not succeeded. I wish the current generation of anthropologists well, and I hope their increased visibility will improve their effectiveness in designing and implementing public policy based on anthropological precepts of social justice. But, I wonder . . .

Note

Acknowledgments. These remarks about his work as an anthropologist in the White House were written as an editorial for one of the first issues of *Practicing Anthropology* (Volume 1, Number 3, February 1979, p. 3 and pp. 23–24). We are particularly pleased to be able to include them in this volume since none of Philleo Nash's colleagues from those days could share his or her recollections with us in 1988. The editorial is reproduced with permission.

Philleo Nash: The Education of an Applied Anthropologist

Fred Eggan

Philleo Nash was born in Wisconsin Rapids in 1909. He was initially interested in music and spent a year at the Curtis Institute of Music in Philadelphia before returning to the University of Wisconsin at Madison where he entered the Meiklejohn Experimental College and then majored in anthropology. As he says in a recent memoir, "I was lucky enough to be one of Ralph Linton's first students at the University of Wisconsin; Lauriston Sharp and Sol Tax were just ahead of me" (1986a). Linton was a charismatic teacher who had come to Madison from the Field Museum in Chicago to develop a program in anthropology, and he had added Charlotte Gower to the department. As Philleo notes, his own professional life came of age with "acculturation" and "applied anthropology," in which both Linton and Gower were concerned, and it may have been Charlotte Gower who influenced him to go to the University of Chicago for graduate work in 1932.

At Chicago, Fay-Cooper Cole and Edward Sapir had been developing a graduate program in anthropology as part of the expansion of the Social Science Divisional activities, and had added Robert Redfield to the department before separating from Sociology in 1929. Redfield, along with Linton, was a pioneer in the study of acculturation, and his thesis on "Tepoztlan, a Mexican Village" had recently been published. Sapir had just gone to Yale, but A. R. Radcliffe-Brown, who had come as a visiting professor, had stayed to develop social anthropology and the comparative study of social systems. In addition, a young political scientist, Harold Lasswell, who had collaborated with Sapir and who was interested in psychoanalysis and political process, became an important influence on Philleo's research.

The American Indians, scattered on reservations mainly in the West, were the traditional groups for anthropological study in the 1930s. John Collier, who had been the major proponent of reform in the activities of the Bureau of Indian Affairs, was appointed Commissioner of Indian Affairs by President Roosevelt in 1933, and the Indian Reorganization Act was passed by Congress in 1934, which brought about major changes on the reservations. In this same year Philleo received a field training fellowship to join a Laboratory of Anthropology group of students to study the Klamath Indian Reservation in Oregon under the direction of Leslie Spier. Here, three different tribes—Klamath, Modoc, and Paviotso—had been put together on the same reservation in the mid-19th century to make farmers out of hunters and gatherers, and each tribe had been differentially affected by the Ghost Dance movement of the 1870s. Philleo had been interested in the Ghost Dance of 1890 and other religious revivalism movements, and had come to the tentative conclusion that nativistic cults arose among deprived groups. Discovering a cache of documents in storage at the Klamath Agency, he determined to investigate what had happened on the Klamath reservation.

In 1935–36 Philleo returned to the reservation as a Predoctoral Fellow of the Social Science Research Council to study "Revivalism and Social Change." He married Edith Rosenfels, a fellow graduate student, in November 1935, and Edith participated in the field research as it continued. During the following year Philleo wrote and defended his thesis and received his Ph.D. in 1937, at the same time preparing a summary chapter for *The Social Anthropology of North American Tribes,* a volume presented to A. R. Radcliffe-Brown on the occasion of his accepting the chair of Social Anthropology at Oxford University. Philleo's chapter, "The Place of Religious Revivalism in the Formation of the Intercultural Community on the Klamath Reservation," began with a hypothesis as to how nativistic cults arise among deprived groups, presented the complicated history of the Klamath, Modoc, and Paviotso tribes before and during the phases of the Ghost Dance activities of 1871–78, and concluded with a revised hypothesis for further testing. The hypothesis came in part from Lasswell, and Lasswell played an important role in monitoring the thesis, but the comparative setting was considerably influenced by Radcliffe-Brown, and the chapter is a fitting tribute to his teaching. Here was a new "model" for the study of acculturation and religious revivals.

Philleo's first academic job was at the University of Toronto, where he was Lecturer in Anthropology and Assistant Keeper of the Ethnological Collections of the Royal Ontario Museum, a position that involved his earlier archeological training under Linton. Here their two children were born and Philleo was well started on an academic career. In 1941 he returned to the family cranberry business and the University of Wisconsin as a lecturer; but with the outbreak of World War II, on the recommendation of Lasswell, he went to work in the Office of Facts and Figures, later the Office of War Information, which carried out opinion and media content analysis and monitored rumors and wartime tensions for the federal government. Many of these arose from the fact that the war had brought increasing numbers of blacks and Hispanics into northern industrial centers, such as Chicago and Detroit, and racial frictions were beginning to turn into riots.

In the course of carrying out his responsibilities, Philleo came in contact with Jonathan Daniels, editor of a North Carolina newspaper, who was in the process of moving into the White House staff as an administrative assistant. Daniels was concerned with the same problems that Philleo was working on and they formed an alliance to keep the government informed of all such developments. During this period Philleo played an important role in helping create the American Council on Race Relations, a private effort funded by several foundations. He also prepared the plan for a network of federal agencies to coordinate efforts to prevent violence in the war industries, which was approved by the president.

With the end of the war, President Truman determined to retain the wartime advances in integration and established the President's Committee on Civil Rights in 1946. David K. Niles had taken Daniels's place as an administrative assistant, and Philleo worked with him, and eventually took his place in the Truman White House. A toughly worded Committee Report (Nash 1947) on segregation and its consequences criticized not only relations between blacks and whites but the evacuation of Japanese Americans from the West Coast and the governing of the Canal Zone and Puerto Rico as well as other territories and provided recommendations for implementation. The civil rights program was underway.

With the end of Truman's term as president, Philleo returned to Wisconsin and Democratic Party politics and his family's cranberry company. He ran for Lieutenant Governor of Wisconsin in 1958 and won the election but was defeated for reelection in 1960. The following year he was appointed Commissioner of Indian Affairs by President Kennedy, after having served on a Task Force on Indian Affairs chaired by W. W. Keeler, with James Officer, William Zimmerman, and Acting Commissioner John Crow as fellow members. Philleo was ultimately nominated by the president to be the new commissioner, and after a spirited Senate confirmation hearing, served from 1961–66.

During the earlier Eisenhower administration, Congress had passed a resolution favoring termination of the reservation system and the ultimate abolishment of the Bureau of Indian Affairs, and several tribes including the Menominee had been terminated. Relocation of Indians from reservations to jobs in major cities had also been undertaken on a large scale. But both of these operations ultimately failed and the Task Force had recommended a change. The later Menominee Restoration Act symbolized the change in attitude of both the country and the Congress.

Once Philleo was confirmed as commissioner he set about implementing the recommendations of the Task Force, including the reversal of termination. For the first time "Applied Anthropology" was not a "dirty word" in the Senatorial committees dealing with Indian affairs. Philleo worked hard to reestablish confidence between the Indians and the BIA, and to organize meetings on reservations with Indian groups. Efforts to develop reservation resources took the place of relocation as economic policy. Philleo once told me he was proudest of providing schools on the reservations for the greatly increased Indian school population and making them as good as neighboring public schools, and sometimes better.

With the death of President Kennedy and the administration of President Johnson, the atmosphere changed, and Philleo was eventually forced to resign as commissioner. He was the first to have the professional qualifications for the position, and he had a realistic view of life on the reservations and what could be done to improve it. But knowing what to do does not always succeed in a political world. As he notes in his 1986 article:

> The U.S. Congress . . . had no interest in anthropology and its application when I was Commissioner. If anything, its members who served on committees active in Indian Affairs, viewed anthropologists as persons who stood in the way of incorporating Indians into the mainstream. Those values which we anthropologists take for granted—cultural identity, cultural pluralism, and cultural diversity—appear to most Western Senators and Congressmen as negatives to the development of their resources. [1986a]

Somewhat disillusioned but still optimistic with regard to the importance of applied anthropology, Philleo remained in Washington as a consultant for development and other programs. In the 1970s he renewed his activities in professional organizations and in the teaching of applied anthropology. He served as president of the Society for Applied Anthropology in 1970–71 and began an association with American University that lasted until his retirement as Professor Emeritus in 1977. The location of American University in Washington and its programs in political and international affairs provided an appropriate setting for his outstanding talents and experience in the use of anthropology in politics and government administration. The anthropology department had already begun an applied program, and Philleo extended its scope in new directions. He brought Margaret Mead to the campus for lectures and after her death organized a special symposium to celebrate her legacy. From his interests in anthropology and education he joined Charles Ferster, a psychologist and educator, in organizing and directing an innovative Learning Center that provided special opportunities for students to structure their own academic progress.

His academic contribution to applied anthropology and his achievements in public affairs were honored by two awards—the Distinguished Service Award of the American Anthropological Association in 1984, and the Malinowski Award of the Society for Applied Anthropology in 1986, which is given in recognition of efforts to understand and serve the needs of the world through social science. He brought new dimensions to the field of anthropology and provided a model of how the anthropological life might be lived. His memoir, "Science, Politics and Human Values" (1986a), is a text as to what can be accomplished in these fields. We will greatly miss him, but his contributions will stand for all time.

Philleo Nash: Anthropologist as Administrator

James E. Officer

In September of 1961, Dr. Philleo Nash took the oath of office as the 38th Commissioner of Indian Affairs. He was the only anthropologist and the last non-Indian to occupy this post—one of the oldest in the federal executive department. He inherited direction of an agency that had a budget in excess of $125 million and employed more than 14,000 persons in locations reaching from Point Barrow, Alaska, to Ft. Lauderdale, Florida, and from Washington, D.C., to the Pacific coast.

Although the position of commissioner was one he had sought as far back as Truman's administration, Nash recognized that he lacked experience in directing such a large, complex organization and he turned to close friends for advice. Among those whom he consulted was William W. Keeler, chief executive officer of the Phillips Petroleum Company. Keeler, principal chief of the Cherokees, had been the chairman of the Indian affairs task force on which Nash had served prior to his appointment, and was one of his strongest boosters.

Among the suggestions Keeler made was that the commissioner create an "operating committee" composed of the upper-level administrators in the Washington office who would meet on a regular—even a daily—basis to review policy and to address problems of bureauwide concern. Keeler had organized a similar body for the corporation he headed, and had found it an effective tool for keeping himself and his immediate subalterns informed about a wide range of matters.

Not long after being sworn in, Nash set up his operating committee, which soon took on the flavor of his personal administrative style. The committee met every day when the commissioner was in Washington unless there was a major emergency to be confronted. It seldom met when Nash was out of town.

The core group for the operating committee included the deputy and associate commissioners, the directors of the major divisions, the congressional liaison officer, the public relations officer, and the economic adviser. Depending on the nature of the agenda, Nash invited others to be present as well. BIA branch chiefs and field officers often attended, as did representatives of other government agencies and of the Indian tribes. Occasionally a congressman or congressional staff member might sit in.

Meetings were characterized by a great deal of give and take and no one who wanted to be heard was denied the opportunity to speak. There was never a vote of any kind; rather, the commissioner—usually following additional consultation with his two closest associates—would make his decision. In a 1986 memoir Nash recalled the operating committee as a useful tool in keeping him informed as to "what was in the minds" of his associates (1986a:198).

Initially, the core members of the committee welcomed the opportunity to exchange views with their colleagues and with the commissioner, but as they became more acquainted with their responsibilities and more absorbed by them, some began to view the operating committee as a drain on their time. In his 1986 address to the Society for Applied Anthropology, Nash recalled that Si Fryer (E.

Reesman Fryer)—the Assistant Commissioner for Economic Development—and I were the members who put the greatest pressure on him to discontinue the operating committee. Both Fryer and I traveled more than most of our colleagues, and I have vivid memories of the extra work it took to get ready to leave Washington and then to catch up after returning. In such circumstances, I sometimes found the two-hour operating committee sessions an annoyance.

Nash felt that giving up the operating committee was a mistake and that his leadership of the bureau weakened after he did away with it. He commented further that if he were ever again to manage a large organization, he would establish such a group. The fact of the matter is, all of us—Fryer included—missed the daily sessions after Philleo abolished them, and both horizontal and vertical communication within the bureau may well have suffered. We should, perhaps, have urged the commissioner to put a time limit on the meetings, or to hold them less regularly rather than cancel them altogether.

Nash's administrative strategy when he took office was to work insofar as possible through the existing structure of the Indian Bureau and to add outsiders primarily in specialized positions related to helping develop and implement new policies. He explained this strategy as follows in a 1966 interview with a representative of the Kennedy library:

> I wanted the position and title of Associate Commissioner for Jim Officer, a friend and confidant of the Secretary and a member of the task force; it was very important to have a suitable spot for him. At the same time, I wanted the old timers, the pros in the Bureau, to be well represented. Therefore, I strongly urged the appointment of John Crow as Deputy Commissioner . . . here we had, you see, the old and the new in a blend which was intended to combine the good things of both for the advancement of the program. It was a good concept and it's been a very successful one. [Morrissey 1966:42]

Prior to Nash's appointment Crow had served as acting commissioner, and old line BIA-ers were rooting for him to become the first confirmed commissioner in history to emerge from their ranks. They openly expressed disappointment at Secretary Udall's choice of Nash, whom they viewed as a clone of former commissioner John Collier. They could not have been more surprised when, at the time of his swearing in, Nash announced that he had asked Crow to be his deputy and that John had accepted.

Following Nash's confirmation and the appointment of Crow and the present writer as his closest associates, Nash announced the convening of a conference of reservation superintendents in Denver. Held in October 1961, it was the first such meeting in nearly a quarter of a century and it gave the commissioner an opportunity to introduce both his new policy and his new administrative team. Secretary Udall and Assistant Secretary Carver also attended. Although there would be confrontations over the next few years between the commissioner and a handful of field officers who could not adapt to his policies and procedures, the Denver meeting signaled the beginning of a new rapport between Nash and those who represented him in reservation and regional offices. The level of that rapport would rise steadily until the end of his tenure as commissioner.

Nash's strategy of combining the old with the new did not set well with some of his closest friends—including a few representatives of the anthropology community. They felt he should have carried out a thorough housecleaning to begin with; then established an applied anthropology unit, similar to the one employed by John Collier. Philleo, however, realized that many of the BIA employees were technicians and professionals—not policymakers—who could be persuaded to follow new directions, provided these were clearly enunciated.

As for the matter of establishing an applied anthropology unit, Nash commented in a paper written in 1970 that he did not do so because "the long-range benefits of the Indian Reorganization Act . . . had in part outdated the need for it." He then pointed out that while the 1930s had "seen experts devising programs to aid beneficiaries" the 1960s would see Indians devising programs for themselves (1970:5–6). Nash did, in fact, bring some anthropologists into the bureau for specialized jobs—among them, Gordon Macgregor who had served with Collier—and he often assigned me responsibilities that called upon my training as an anthropologist. I spent many weeks in the field—at such places as Fort Hall in Idaho, the native communities of Alaska, and small fishing villages of western Washington—carrying out tasks that most of us would characterize as applied anthropology.

Nash constantly stressed the importance of BIA personnel and Indians working together. When he was in the field, he insisted that BIA officials be invited to public meetings he held with tribal members. While he was willing to listen in private to the complaints of tribal leaders against local bureau personnel, he did not allow public meetings to degenerate into attacks on them. If he was convinced that a local official could not work with a particular tribe, he found a way to transfer that individual to another position, but he did not jump immediately to move a superintendent because a tribal councilman or chairman did not like him. Nash's evenhandedness with both Indians and BIA employees resulted eventually in a much better working relationship between the two.

Early in his administration, Nash began to seek the collaboration of other government agencies in providing more and better services for reservation communities and in promoting economic development. From the outset, he made clear his desire for the Indians to deal directly with these agencies rather than to rely upon the bureau as an intermediary. He was willing to have BIA representatives attend planning meetings and conduct orientation sessions, but he balked at having them play additional roles. When Indians came to him with complaints about programs administered by other agencies, Nash informed them as to the appropriate officials within those agencies to whom such complaints should be presented; and when agency representatives asked him to intervene with tribes, he referred them to tribal leaders. Eventually, several federal bureaus and departments established liaision offices staffed with persons accustomed to doing business with Indians.

Nash's political skills and sensitivity stood him in good stead in dealing with these kinds of situations. He could sense when playing the broker's role might result in further criticism of the Indian Bureau, and he was careful to avoid being caught in the middle.

I recall one incident where he wisely counseled me to stay on the sidelines in a dispute between some of the Indians of California and their claims attorneys. The lawyers were seeking a compromise in the California claims case and this compromise required the approval of the Indians and of the bureau, as well as of the attorneys representing the U.S. government. At some of the meetings held to determine Indian views, meetings which the Claims Commission insisted the BIA conduct, a majority of those present voted against the compromise. Fearful that the proposed settlement might be rejected, the attorneys asked whether I would authorize a mail ballot in view of the fact that the percentage of Indians attending the meetings was quite low.

Because I knew the bureau would eventually have to certify to the Claims Commission that the Indians had been given full opportunity to accept or reject the proposed compromise, I gave serious consideration to changing the procedures so as to provide for a written expression of Indian opinion. Philleo, however, argued that the involvement of the BIA was already much greater than it should be and the Claims Commission, rather than the Indian Bureau, should decide whether to allow absentee ballots. I took his advice and informed the attorneys of our decision. At their urging, the Commission did change the voting procedures, an action that angered many Indians and eventually produced a lawsuit. For a change, the BIA was not the target of the attack.

Nash was one of history's most effective commissioners when it came to dealing with the appropriations committees of Congress. He succeeded not only in doubling the budget of the BIA, but also in helping other federal agencies increase many fold the monies they received to conduct programs on the reservations. His success was due in large part to the care he gave to preparing for budget hearings. I can recall the many hours we spent with the heads of the various divisions and branches, learning from them the facts and statistics we would need to answer anticipated questions. Nash committed much of this material to memory and often surprised congressmen and their staff assistants by his ability to answer some of their most complex inquiries without turning to his own helpers for assistance.

Given his facility for dealing with senators and representatives on the appropriations committees, it is difficult to explain why Nash's relations with certain members and staff personnel of the legislative subcommittees on Indian affairs should have remained cool throughout his term and eventually contributed to the request for his resignation. Philleo himself might have had an answer for this enigma, but he never confided it to me, nor have I encountered it in his writing. One explanation might be that he was simply plagued with bad luck. At the time Nash took over the office of commissioner, Clinton P. Anderson of New Mexico was the most powerful member of the Senate Interior Committee. From the outset, he chided those of us on the task force for not endorsing termination as the major goal of federal Indian policy, and he appeared to blame Philleo for the fact that we did not do so. Jim Gamble, an appointee of Senator Anderson who was the principal staff member on Indian affairs in the Senate, was an outspoken terminationist and equally outspoken as a critic of Commissioner Nash.

Also involved in Philleo's relationship with the Senate was the fact that he could not deliver Indian endorsement for a bill favored by Senator Church to solve the so-called "heirship" problem that is a legacy of the general allotment act of 1887. In later years Nash would conclude that legislation was not needed to control this problem, but he did work hard for its enactment. Church was so unhappy with its failure to pass that he resigned as chairman of the Indian Affairs Subcommittee and seemed thereafter to harbor a certain bitterness toward the commissioner.

Senator Henry Jackson of Washington, who replaced Anderson as head of the Interior Committee, clashed with Nash on at least two major issues. One had to do with the fishing rights of the Indians of the Pacific Northwest. Although initially friendly to the Indians' point of view, Jackson came increasingly to favor the position of the sports fishermen of the state who were calling for a "buyout" of Indian treaty fishing rights. Following the lead of the Indians, Nash opposed any such arrangement.

The commissioner and the senator also crossed swords on the issue of terminating the Colville reservation. Some of Jackson's close supporters were Colvilles living away from the reservation who favored division of tribal assets and an end to federal trusteeship and special services. Senator Jackson became the agent of these Indians in promoting a two-step termination plan that frightened the on-reservation Colvilles and the Indians of many other tribes. Nash, who was well aware of Indian sentiment generally, did not give this matter the kind of priority that the senior senator from Washington felt it deserved.

While Nash was battling key senators over some of these issues, Secretary of the Interior Udall was promoting major conservation legislation that required the support of the same individuals. Udall apparently came to believe that Nash's relations with these elected officials might prejudice the outcome of bills affecting other agencies under his jurisdiction. Although the secretary was a personal friend of mine and I saw him socially as well as professionally, he did not tell me of his plans for seeking Philleo's resignation until after he met with him and requested it.

On the other hand, I had known that Udall was disappointed with what he regarded as slow progress in improving the economic situation on the reservations. He, also, did not feel he had the close relationship with Nash that he enjoyed with other bureau chiefs within the department. At my urging he suggested to the commissioner that he come up to his office at least once a week to meet with him. The commissioner later told me that when he tried to do so, he was often blocked by the secretary's administrative assistant and found himself spending literally hours in the outer office awaiting his turn. He found this experience humiliating and abandoned the effort.

When Nash's departure was announced in 1966, many of the employees of the BIA who five years earlier thought he would be a disaster as commissioner felt a sense of despair; and Indian leaders throughout the country expressed their displeasure both publicly and privately. Some of their feelings are contained in letters of condolence that Mrs. Nash received following Philleo's death. One from a national Indian leader conveys the feelings of many when he stated that "Philleo was certainly good to me when I was a naive young man . . . he made it possible for me to continue in the NCAI and build it up to more than 150 tribal memberships before I left . . . I certainly couldn't have done the job without him."

And a former employee of the BIA wrote,

> In June 1975, while I was still area director in Billings, Philleo was here for a speech. We had an office party one night, and he had a great time renewing old friendships. Later in the evening I was looking for him, and found him sitting with a group of young Indian employees, who had come into the BIA well after his term. He was having a seminar on Indian policy, and they were all debating some tough questions. The next week I talked to some of the participants, and have always remembered the one who said, 'now we know what a real commissioner is like.'

Philleo Nash and American Indian People

Nancy Oestreich Lurie

I don't recall when I first met Philleo, but it was in connection with our mutual concern for the Wisconsin Winnebago that we became good friends. Philleo was acquainted with the tribe from his boyhood because he grew up in central Wisconsin where the cranberry industry employed many Winnebago people. My introduction to the Wisconsin Winnebago was during the cherry harvest of 1944 in Door County, Wisconsin, the thumblike peninsula that juts into Lake Michigan, where I did my first fieldwork as an undergraduate (Lurie 1972).

At that time, the Wisconsin Winnebago economy was based on a seasonal itinerary. They had no reservation because they had refused to leave Wisconsin with the more southerly bands of the tribe who eventually obtained a reservation in Nebraska. In 1874, the Wisconsin Winnebago were allowed to take up Indian homesteads held in federal trust for individuals rather than in tribal trust like a reservation. They settled more or less as regional bands in the vicinity of the towns of Wittenberg, Wisconsin Rapids, Black River Falls, Tomah, Wisconsin Dells, and La Crosse.

The seasonal round began in the spring with wild blueberries and commercially grown strawberries. As July wore on, people left their communities to work for a month or more in "cherryland." Between cherries in midsummer and cranberries in the fall, the two crops on which virtually all families depended for a major part of their annual income, some families harvested potatoes or apples or raised beans or pickles on contract with canneries. When the cranberry season ended, a few people still trapped. In the winter and other slack periods, production of splint basketry was a mainstay for most families.

Philleo probably never anticipated that when he became Commissioner of the Bureau of Indian Affairs (BIA) his old friends, the Wisconsin Winnebago, would pose a special problem for his administration, requiring his personal intervention and resulting in a warm renewal of friendship with the Indian people he had associated with in his youth.

It all began with the American Indian Chicago Conference (AICC) of 1961 when the guiding spirit, Sol Tax, asked me to serve as his assistant (Lurie 1961). AICC followed the principles of Tax's "Action Anthropology" to achieve intertribal consensus on alternatives to the devastating federal policies of the 1950s. An all-Indian steering committee was developed, continuously improved drafts of a basic document were sent to an ever-enlarging mailing list, and regional meetings were held in preparation for the final meeting in Chicago in June of 1961.

The people in the Midwest felt that their region was not adequately represented, and the steering committee readily agreed to add the region's candidate, Helen Miner Miller, a young Wisconsin Winnebago woman who taught business courses in a Chicago suburban high school.

During the period I worked with the Winnebago in the 1940s, they were self-sufficient and independent. By the 1950s they began to experience massive unemployment as crop harvesting became increasingly mechanized. Although a few years of schooling had been sufficient for crop work, many Winnebago lacked skills for other kinds of employment. A good deal of homestead land had been lost in a process similar to the loss of allotments on reservations. Some people lived as squatters on mission and other non-Indian land; most housing was poor and lacked electricity or running water. By 1961, the tribe was in desperate need. When they sought help they often were denied Indian Bureau assistance because of their non-reservation status and were denied public assistance because local welfare offices considered them a BIA responsibility.

Helen and I got together right after AICC to try to develop means of helping the tribe. The first problem was the lack of an organizational structure to coordinate self-help efforts. The tribal communities are separated from each other by no less than 30 miles, and some are more than 100 miles apart. There was interregional distrust and the tribe also was divided, in some cases bitterly, by religious differences between the traditional religion, Native American Church (Peyote), and mission Christianity. There was also a lack of quantified data on the tribe's condition to support any application for community development funding.

On the plus side, we identified a core of about a dozen people who had gone to high school and even beyond or had learned trades and had a certain degree of economic security. They were bilingual, had remained strongly identified as Winnebago, and were representative of all the tribal regions and the three religions. They could serve as the nucleus in organizing for self-help if they were willing to work together as unpaid volunteers. They responded to the idea with enthusiasm at the start and with dedication in the long haul. Helen and I were encouraged by the recent appointment of Philleo Nash as Indian Commissioner, both because he had attended the AICC as part of a team appointed by Interior Secretary Stewart Udall to consult with Indians across the country, and because he was personally well acquainted with the Wisconsin Winnebago.

It soon became clear that the best foundation for coordinating tribal action to qualify for development programs was the Indian Reorganization Act of 1934 (IRA). In response to Helen's inquiry, the BIA ruled that since the tribe had not actually voted against the IRA when it was promoted in Indian country in 1935–37, they still were eligible to organize and benefit from its provisions. Helen and the group she attracted to work with her began studying IRA guidelines to develop a constitution and bylaws, designating themselves the Acting Wisconsin Winnebago Business Committee (WWBC). Following the pattern of AICC, the group developed a tribal mailing list to circulate drafts, which were then discussed at regional meetings. To assure total tribal comprehension and to gather any final input, the third and last draft was translated phrase by phrase into Winnebago at a general meeting. Besides satisfying the tribe, the document met the full and admiring approval of the local BIA adviser who was asked to review it before it was submitted to the Washington office in the spring of 1962.

As work wound down on the constitution, Helen and I turned to the second problem, the need for data to plan programs. Helen and the Acting WWBC had already contributed as much as they could afford to developing the constitution, and we needed money to bring the WWBC *cum* Research Team together to develop a survey instrument, meet regularly to compile and compare results, buy supplies, and, above all, pay for mileage and some incidental expenses for the team to contact the widely scattered Indian households.

I offered to apply for a scholarly grant, but Helen quite rightly insisted that it had to be awarded to the tribe as a first step in developing confidence and responsibility in money management and self-help. We worked up a prospectus and sent it out to dozens of private and public agencies. When we got replies at all, they were negative. We could read between the lines: Indians were a poor risk. On November 2, 1962, our only positive response finally came from the Social Security Administration, then under the Department of Health, Education, and Welfare, which had a small fund for programs for "preventing dependency." Mr. HEW GRANT, as it was promptly named, provided $7331 and required a match of about $3000 from the applicant. Eventually, it was more than matched in volunteer hours, but the project was delayed in getting underway until early in 1963 because of a dreadful development.

The tribe had expected rapid authorization from the BIA to hold the required referendum to formally accept the constitution, but no word was received until late in the fall of 1962. The Solicitor General's Office that has to review such authorization requests ruled that the Wisconsin Winnebago did not qualify under IRA after all. Helen appealed directly to Philleo by telegram and I followed up with a detailed letter on November 24. Philleo took personal action to get the tribe's request reconsidered and wrote to me on December 4: "As of today the train is again back on the track. Three days ago the Associate Solicitor overruled his subordinates and held that there was not a legal impediment to the approval of the Winnebago Constitution, and we telephoned Helen Miner Miller. . . ."

Although not detailed in his letter, what had happened was that a nonreservation tribe had been held ineligible for IRA in 1947, and this was used as a precedent. Philleo's insistence on a review of the decision resulted in the discovery that many years earlier an old Winnebago had died without known heirs. As a matter of expediency, the BIA had declared the homestead tribal trust land—only 40 acres, but the tribe had a "reservation." I am sure that even if this fluke had not occurred, Philleo would have found some other way around a ruling from the period when the government was beginning to consider terminating federal responsibility to tribes.

The BIA calculated from its skimpy data and the tribe's mailing list that there were 494 eligible voters. Almost 100 people would have to vote to have a valid referendum, and passage would require 75 votes. When the referendum was held on January 19, 1963, 522 Wisconsin Winnebago proved eligible to cast ballots; 514 voted in favor of the constitution, 5 voted against, and 3 ballots were invalid for technical reasons. A remarkable demonstration of the communication developed throughout the tribe in two years is that there were 171 absentee ballots that had to be requested and notarized from Winnebago living away from communities where polling places were set up. IRA status was officially conferred on March 19, and on June 8, officers were elected to the business committee, with Helen Miller serving as the first tribal chairperson.

While working on the HEW survey during the summer of 1963, the WWBC began taking action as problems came to their attention: getting Indian children on free hot lunch programs, helping people fill out forms for public assistance, qualifying for a surplus food distribution center.

The first General Council was held on September 14 at the powwow grounds at Black River Falls. Philleo arrived in a chartered plane at the little local airport. He took time from his busy schedule to accept the tribe's invitation because he *wanted* to share in the joy of the occasion. When it was his turn to speak, he noted that the awarding of BIA scholarships had been confined to reservation residents, but this was a matter of policy, not law. Henceforth, the far flung Wisconsin Winnebago could apply for educational funding like other IRA tribes. I happened to be looking in the direction of the head of the Wisconsin BIA office and will never forget the expression on his face. He had come up through a bureaucracy oriented since the end of World War II to finding excuses for serving as few Indians as possible.

Thanks to Philleo's directive and WWBC follow-up, by the next year the Winnebago had jumped from the bottom to the top of the list of Wisconsin tribes in regard to the number of students in colleges and technical schools. Philleo also expedited Wisconsin Winnebago efforts to add more land to tribal trust status, something unheard of since the administration of John Collier, to enable them to qualify for housing requiring a tribal land base. He saw to it that they got a housing project as soon as the first land was acquired.

Of course, Philleo took personal interest in tribal aspirations and plans across the country, but the Wisconsin Winnebago case is of special interest because he moved fast to keep Indian faith in tribal government when he recognized a tribe had agreed on what they wanted to do. He also was sensitive to the need to allow time for tribes to achieve fully informed consensus before embarking on major community development projects and recognized that sociocultural differences among tribes had to be respected if the Bureau was to work effectively with them. I think it was impatience with Philleo's sensitivity, deemed inefficiency by those above him in the government, that finally forced him out of office by 1966.

His wisdom about the need for patience and time for adequate communication was demonstrated in an ironical way when the Wisconsin Winnebago decided, after much discussion in 1965–66, to tap into the Great Lakes Intertribal program of the Office of Economic Opportunity (OEO), supposedly designed to encourage grassroots self-help efforts in Lyndon Johnson's "War on Poverty." When the WWBC completed their survey in 1963, statistically documenting the socioeconomic condition of the tribe (Miller and Lurie 1963), HEW volunteered another $7333 to gather more data in regard to program planning, which also allowed some immediate implementation like the first grant. For reasons of health, Helen had to give up her tribal activities in 1964, and her directorship for the grant was continued by Nadine Day Sieber (Sieber and Lurie 1965). The WWBC really had little choice in seeking support for their work when the second grant ran out because after Philleo left office, OEO virtually supplanted the BIA as a major source of funding for Indian programs during the Johnson administration.

Armed with their survey publications, the new tribal government, and a sense of unity and purpose, the WWBC and tribe at large recognized that they had already laid the kind of grassroots foundation that OEO required Indian and other communities to carry out in preparation for community action. The Wisconsin Winnebago were ready for action and knew what they needed: funding they would manage as they had managed their grants to continue programs begun with HEW money, such as the tribal newssheet and mileage for WWBC officers to maintain intratribal communication; other programs begun with their own now very thin shoestrings; and funding for projects they had planned as a tribe.

Their surveys were disregarded and they were expected to do the grassroots thing according to OEO guidelines, which didn't include tribal newssheets. They got no funding, just ready-made programs managed by OEO and designed for Wisconsin's compact reservation communities. Travel funds were available only for outside experts to come and advise the WWBC, not for tribal officers to conduct tribal business. They got Head Start but no money for educational programs they had begun to keep older students in school and encourage post–high school education. Winnebago program workers got instructions from and were answerable only to the OEO administrators, not the tribal government.

By 1969, OEO had very nearly undone all that the tribe had accomplished on its own. They still are struggling to overcome the effects of schisms, revival of old regional and religious antagonisms, blame casting, and communication breakdowns engendered during the OEO period. As they struggle to regain stability and control over their affairs, they continue to honor the legacy of Philleo's efforts.

Celebrating Philleo's Life

Ada Deer

In keeping with the Indian tradition, what you read here is not based on a manuscript. I like to talk and I like to feel what an audience is conveying. During my talk I could feel the encirclement of Philleo, his spirit, his zest, his energy.

I first met Philleo when, as a young social worker in Minneapolis in the early 1960s, I had the opportunity to come East for a social work meeting. This was in New York only one year after I had completed my graduate education, so I thought, "Well, it's about time that I touched base with Washington." I knew that the Bureau of Indian Affairs was there and it was a big, important bureaucracy for Indian people and so I picked up the phone when I came to Washington and called his office and told them that I was a young social worker, a member of the Menominee tribe, working in Minneapolis, and I was interested in meeting the commissioner and talking with him. Now the person who answered the phone asked if I had met him before or if he knew me. I said, "No, but he will," and he did. It turned out that he was quite busy, but if I came at a certain time I could. (I liked to tease Philleo later that he had ten minutes between elevators.) Actually it was a few minutes between some of his meetings, but I thought this was a good indication of his openness, his receptivity, his willingness to meet people.

When I met with him, I told him that I had just started working in Minneapolis at one of the neighborhood centers and that one of the reasons I worked there and had not gone elsewhere across the country was because at that time there were very few trained Indian graduate social workers. One of the reasons I had chosen the Midwest was because that was my home area and also this neighborhood house had an Indian program. During my year there I had become more familiar with a number of the urban Indian problems and I wanted to talk with him about them. So he said okay. And we chatted and I told him that I thought that a lot of the Indian people were brought into the cities unprepared, that the city agencies felt that this was the responsibility of the Bureau of Indian Affairs and that the county also was not willing to assist since these Indians weren't on reservations. (I knew about the relocation program but I didn't have a complete analysis of it at the time.) I just informed him that I thought the Bureau of Indian Affairs should. He smiled at me and we talked and he said that he would be in touch. This was in 1964.

The next time that I was touched by Philleo, I got a call from the director of the Minneapolis Area Office, who at that time was Mr. James Hawkins. It turned out, as I found out later, that this was at the instruction of Philleo. At the time I thought, oh well, it's about time I did meet the area director and start talking and so on. At any rate, I learned that, after discussing the urban Indian situation at that time, Philleo thought, "Well, we ought to bring this young woman into the Bureau of Indian Affairs." And so he had created this position called Community Services Coordinator. It was a very interesting position and I interpreted it as a special assistant to the area director. I had a lot of freedom to meet with a lot of groups in the Minneapolis area and the surrounding states of Minnesota, Iowa, Wisconsin, and I helped interpret the bureau's programs as well as develop a much greater and much deeper understanding of Indian problems in my area. I was also present at the time that Philleo was adopted into the Minnesota Chippewa tribe. This happened in the early 1960s at Red Lake. This was a very memorable occasion.

Now, I had no intention of working for the bureau, but as you can see I ended up working for the bureau. It was a very interesting experience. It had a great deal of influence on my understanding of how bureaucracies work. Of course, my experience was quite different from that of many people in the bureau because I started out first by calling the commissioner and telling him what I thought. And I should tell you that I didn't know it at the time but my mother, who has recently died, had started writing to Philleo. She was a white woman (I teased her; I told her she was an Indian in a previous life) who had a great sense of social justice and she started writing to Philleo about the injustice of termination that had been brought on the Menominee tribe. I know that she was a very stubborn person, a very strong-minded person, and her letters are often very blunt and sharp. And so to Philleo's credit, despite the fact that my name was Deer and he knew that she was my mother, he agreed to see me and then brought me into the bureau. So this was my early experience with Philleo as a young Indian woman, a professional. Then, working in the bureau, I had the opportunity to see the reaction of other Indian people to him.

It was a wonderful experience that day at Red Lake. This was a day that was organized by Roger Jourdain and the other Chippewa tribal members. It was a wonderful occasion. There was a full dress made according to Philleo's measurements, and Philleo entered into the occasion with his usual zest and energy and spoke movingly and with his usual deep respect and appreciation and enjoyment of the Indian rituals and ceremonies.

The next time that my life was touched in a great manner by Philleo was in 1966. I worked in the bureau from about 1964 until 1967. Now coming fresh out of graduate school, I wanted to be a professional, so I decided that I should write a report in a reasonable amount of time. What was I doing? Why was I doing it? What were the implications for this? This report turned out to be perhaps 10–15 pages, a very simple report. But I didn't just list activities. I tried to do some analysis, some synopsis. I said, well the governor says this but he does that; the area director says this but this is what happened; the superintendent says this and this is what doesn't happen. And so they felt that this report should be sent on to Washington. Okay, so the report got sent on to Washington. I was then told that after reading this report Philleo felt it would be beneficial for me to improve my understanding of Indian affairs and peoples. So he devised what he called a commissioner's leadership training trip. Now this was somewhat of a mysterious undertaking, I am sure, because the people in the Bureau of Indian Affairs didn't understand what the purpose was and why I had been selected. It was a wonderful experience for me. I spent several months in the Southwest. I had these nice government travel tickets and I could devise my own plan, which I did. I didn't know very much about the Indians of the Southwest, and Philleo announced to me that it was time that I learned about Indians other than in my own area. So he got me into the habit that I am still carrying on today: "Have passport, will travel."

I had a tremendous educational and professional experience, and learned much there from my Indian colleagues and friends. This was mystifying to them too because I had a government car and I was an employee of the Bureau of Indian

Affairs, but I was only there to listen and to learn and I didn't want anything from them; I was just there to listen. And so I did. I remember one time in a house in a Pueblo when I visited there for the first time and people were always polite and respectful. They were also curious about meeting other Indians. In my conversation with this one gentleman he said that the Pueblo had been there since the time before Columbus and I said, yes, I knew that they had a very long tradition and that they had much to be proud of. And I enjoyed meeting them and learning. Now the question was: "What kind of life would the people have in the future?" "Well, I noticed that you don't have electricity here and is this something that you will continue to do? Has your tribal council thought about this? The youngsters can't study after the sun goes down." And he says, "Hm, how come other people don't talk to us like this?"

These policies and resolutions come down, but again this was an example of the impact that I was able to have but also of the great learnings that I enjoyed through this trip. In later years Philleo said that that was the best $5000 he ever spent. The reason that I tell you this is that in my life and in the life of my family, it illustrates how Philleo reached out and touched and brought in, recognized the talent and the ability, the leadership capabilities in people. In his position as commissioner he then made it possible for me, and I am sure for other people too, to develop their own talent and abilities and to further the cause of Indian people. So at the end of the 1966 training trip, there was another little report. But by that time Philleo was gone, and nothing happened to that report. Now that was a longer report and I made a few observations. I felt that the bureau was such a large organization that there was not as much communication as there could have been or should have been. That there should be a lot more emphasis on the development of the leadership of Indian people. There were some other recommendations, too. But I decided I would wait for a while and if nothing happened, then I was going to leave. Well, nothing happened and so I decided to leave, and I left. Of course, I wasn't through with my contacts with Philleo, because once a person like Philleo enters your life, your life is never the same and you check in for a while and then you may check out, but the influence and the circle of friendship continues.

Now during all of this time this knowledge and skills and the understanding that I obtained through my work with the Bureau of Indian Affairs, I've used in my subsequent work. In 1969 we started working on restoration of the Menominee tribe. One of the first persons that I went to see was Philleo Nash. My lawyer and I went to visit him in Wisconsin Rapids and spent a number of hours discussing this whole operation before it began, because I knew that Philleo had the knowledge and the wisdom and the perspective that would be necessary. We knew that this would be a huge effort. But without consultation from Philleo and getting his perspective on this we felt we wouldn't be able to proceed effectively. So we had a long discussion with him. He did say that it would be difficult. It was a terrible injustice, the termination. So he became a very active consultant in this whole restoration effort. We started the effort and that's another whole story, but I want to say that throughout this he was my friend, my mentor. He was my consultant; he opened up his heart, his home. When people asked me where I was living in Washington, I would sometimes be a little reluctant to tell them, because we had the hospitality of the Nashes in their Washington residence, and it was a very lovely place. Occasionally, people like LaDonna Harris (president of Americans for Indian Opportunity) would come over and occasionally, when we couldn't arrange for housing, some of our people would stay.

The Menominee Restoration Act was successful and one of the reasons this was successful was the knowledge and skill that I had obtained through my contact and work in the Bureau of Indian Affairs and through the support and faith and the concrete assistance that Philleo gave. Lots of people want to help Indians. Usually this means they want to tell you what to do, but in Philleo's case he would listen and give his advice and then help in very concrete ways. After the restoration effort—I too am somewhat of a political person—and in my campaign for Secretary of State for Wisconsin, Edith and Philleo Nash actively supported me, gave a wonderful fundraiser at their home in Wisconsin Rapids, and contributed financially to those efforts.

The next major time that I had with Philleo was in Sun Valley, Idaho. I have a picture of this conference in 1984, fifty years after the IRA (Indian Restoration Act). It is a beautiful picture, which I shall always cherish, and again it shows Philleo's sense of history. We have Daniel Poler, who is one of the tribal members of Wisconsin. There's Philleo, and then we have Phyllis Frederick, who is a member of the Brotherton; this is a small tribe that is now striving for recognition again. Then we have Robert Bennett, who was the commissioner immediately following Philleo Nash, from Oneida, a career person in the Bureau of Indian Affairs.

I was born in 1935 and I celebrated my 50th birthday in 1985. I decided that since Gloria Steinem had had a big bash at the Waldorf that I would also have a bash. My friends would come and we would raise money for a good cause. And so Philleo came to my 50th birthday party. We had a wonderful time. We had the governor there, various academics, and other Indians and non-Indians, and I am very happy to say that we established a scholarship fund, the Ada Deer Scholarship Fund, and that one of the exciting points was having Philleo there, my mentor, my former employer, my consultant, and most importantly of all, my good friend.

So he's had an impact on me personally. He's had an impact on me professionally. He's had an impact on my tribe, not only in his capacity as Commissioner for Indians; but through his impact on me, he's had additional impact on Indian policy across the country, because I have served as a member of the American Indian Policy Review Commission, and I am currently a member of the executive committee of the Native American Rights Fund. Throughout all this, I keep in mind a model commissioner because he helped me see that government is to be human. It is not to be a rigid bureaucracy that you have to fight through. Since I had such good initial contact with him as the commissioner, I feel that all the people in the government should be like him. I remind them about this. When I was in the Bureau of Indian Affairs, Minneapolis Area Office, I used to tease the secretaries. I would say, "Well, if the commissioner calls, tell him I'm out." Of course they never quite knew what to do with me. One time he did call, and I was out. They had fun with me on that one.

I do have a very positive attitude toward the type of policymaking and operations that Philleo Nash exemplified and carried out. I recently was in Montana and Wyoming. I had the occasion to visit some very old friends, Reginald and Gladys Laubin. They are non-Indians who are experts in many aspects of Indian culture. He, Philleo, put my sister Ferial in touch with the Laubins. My sister Ferial at that time was very interested in dance and Indian culture. So, he has had an impact on my sister Ferial's life. She went down to work at the Institute of American Indian

Arts in Santa Fe and met the Laubins, and now we are busily referring nieces and nephews to the Laubins. The circles of care and concern and compassion continue, not only in me and my sister, but in the younger generations. Philleo visited the Menominee Reservation, my home in Wisconsin, saw our log cabin; he has gone swimming, as has Edith, in the Wolf River. I have gone swimming in the Wisconsin River near their cottage. I have stayed in their home in Washington. We've had a very warm interchange of friendship and love over the years.

As I think back on Philleo's impact I want to emphasize many of his wonderful qualities. First of all his warmth, his openness, his humor (he used to always tell me "Now don't take yourself too seriously"), his sense of humanity, his kinship with all people, but his special kinship to American Indians. His sensitivity. This must be underscored. His zest, his energy, and his love of life expressed each day. Occasionally I would talk to him and I would say, "Well, don't all these bureaucrats get you down?" And he would say, "Yes and no." I would say, "You always seem to be so positive, so energetic." And he would smile and say, "Yes." One time I asked him what the difference was between the administration under John F. Kennedy and under Lyndon Baines Johnson. So he said, "Under Mr. Kennedy, you never knew when the phone rang whether it was him or not, so you had to be on your toes." There was this change when Mr. Johnson came in. He went to his tasks every day at the bureau with the excitement that the telephone would ring and it could be the president, or it could be Ada Deer.

He's made an indelible impression on me personally and professionally. And I have enlarged this circle to my family, to my friends, to my tribe, and to Indians today nationally in many of my efforts. He's renewed me, he's inspired me, he's warmed my heart, he's challenged me in every way. Although he's not here with us physically, we can all feel his presence and I want to close by quoting words of Chief Seattle who said, "There is no death, only a change of worlds." And I know that Philleo is up there advising and applying.

Philleo Nash's Contributions to Anthropology and Beyond at American University

Ruth Landman

By a happy coincidence, in 1970 I learned that Philleo Nash might be persuaded to return to university teaching at a moment when I was a very new department chair in a department that was just starting to offer a concentration in applied anthropology. At that time Gordon MacGregor was about to retire; he had joined our department after a varied career in applied work with the Sioux and other Indian groups, as well as on the rural life studies project of the 1930s and a variety of overseas assignments for the Agency for International Development. In addition, we were becoming the home department for Absolom Vilakazi, whose applied work had largely been done as a social and economic development officer for southern and eastern Africa at the United Nations. He had held a joint appointment at American and Howard Universities initially. Katherine Halpern had already spent a year as a visiting professor in our department, on leave from her position as research director for the Boston University School of Social Work, and had now joined our department permanently. With this core of experienced colleagues we were ready to offer an M.A. in Applied Anthropology. But it was with some trepidation that I approached Philleo, whose roles in the White House, in Wisconsin politics, and at the BIA made me wonder whether I was really overreaching with the suggestion that he might want to join our department, where the doctoral program was only two years old, and all we could offer him was an adjunct appointment.

But we were lucky. Philleo was eager to work with students and full of ideas of how to bring his other experiences to bear on courses and advising individual students. In the seven years that American University was his base, he contributed to the department, the college and the entire university in an extraordinary variety of enterprises.

Let me mention some of them: He joined and, for one year, directed the University Learning Center, an experimental college without walls. To sharpen the special skills and qualities he felt were needed in its integrated program, he enrolled in a Tavistock Institute training program. As he reported:

> The work of the . . . Learning Center is built in part around Home Base Groups . . . My inclination as a teacher, administrator and participant in group discussions before the Amherst conference would naturally have led me . . . to be an active leader, highly directive, reducing things to first principles, and summarizing them for the benefit of my students. This is still my natural tendency (as whose is it not) . . . but ten small group sessions . . . made me more able to restrain myself in the interest of the whole group . . . and to be more task oriented. . . .

Here was Philleo, sixty years old, willing and eager to retrain himself to fit a role with with 1960s students. Simultaneously, he eagerly volunteered to teach a course integrating anthropology, biology and psychology, called "Humankind through Space and Time," in the university's experimental Liberal Studies Program. In this course he decided to use a new series of films made by Asen Belicki as well as a variety of other recently prepared audiovisual materials. Not content with energetically developing this course, oversubscribed by enthusiastic undergraduates, Philleo integrated his work at American University with his longtime interest in the education of children, expressed in the Nash family's founding and leadership roles in Georgetown Day School.

This took the form of arranging to teach "Anthropology for Teachers." The announcement made clear that the class was going to be held at a time of day between teachers' school hours and their private evenings. It was a course that was offered jointly by the anthropology department and the School of Education (showing Philleo's invariable attention to practical matters, because many teachers could thereby serve their credentialing needs), and students were also invited to enroll through the Division of Adult Education if they weren't in a degree program.

Again, I'd like to quote briefly from the course announcement, because the language is so characteristic of Philleo's style:

> In all ways possible, the course is designed to be of service to working teachers, public and private. . . . The course is equally an introduction to the concepts of anthropology and the techniques of multi-media teaching. A full array . . . will be explored, including games and simulations. . . .

I think that Philleo saw his entire role as an anthropologist in the light of the service his chosen field could offer. This gave his view of applied anthropology an optimistic and highly engaged quality. He showed us, as his colleagues and students, how to act within the limits of the possible, and how he felt it was wrong to withdraw from the fray when one's advice is not fully accepted or implemented.

This was apparent in the courses he taught for our department in development anthropology, in applied anthropology, and in the many informal conversations and seminars. He obviously relished being in the midst of action and was an ideal faculty member for our department in its commitment to training applied anthropologists.

The university also recognized this capacity and bent, and asked Philleo Nash to chair a Task Force on Basic Skills. This was at a time when the first national outcry about declining student achievement and educational standards was agitating the academy. Philleo chaired the task force and wrote a vigorous report, which essentially laid out all the steps the university eventually adopted to raise admission and graduation requirements.

I think this pragmatic, optimistic, and can-do outlook was one that made him also an enthusiastic collaborator and publicist for Margaret Mead: it was a quality they shared. At American University this took the form of organizing a weekend Margaret Mead Institute for a group of about thirty participants who came from all over the Mid Atlantic area. And it was during his years here that he joined the board of her Inter-Cultural Institute.

Finally, and very importantly, I want to say something about the quality of Philleo's connection with students and young people more generally. There was a very special chemistry at work, because Philleo had an unusually warm and intense relationship with many of the students and with his friends' children. Jim Bodine recalls the "thunderous applause from the students at commencement when he was made Professor Emeritus, his low wave to them, and those smiling eyes."

Georgetown Day may have been founded on important principles of integration and teaching methods, but it surely also reflects the personal warmth and enthusiasm that Philleo always showed toward children and young people.

While the country would have lost a lot had Philleo devoted his entire life to a university career, I am certain the field of anthropology would have been sprinkled with a network of his former students who would have made a significant mark on the shape of the profession. More of us would have stayed out in the public arena in the late 1940s and 1950s as his A.U. students have indeed done.

Philleo Nash: Model Applied Anthropologist and Public Servant

Pearl Walker-McNeil

It is an honor and a privilege to be counted among those who studied under Philleo Nash. I had been a full-time homemaker, prematurely widowed, who had just emerged from the turbulent 1960s with four teenagers who made it to college. Two followed in the footsteps of their scholarly father and earned doctorates. The younger two preferred vocational studies and early marriage. I returned to graduate school to follow through on a Ph.D. program that had been interrupted.

Dr. Nash taught three courses that were of special interest to me: "Anthropology for Teachers," "Anthropology of Education," and "Anthropology of Development." I was a liberal arts college professor on study leave, so "Anthropology for Teachers" captured my attention. I had a continuing interest in volunteer activities and community service from my homemaker years. My membership in the Parent-Teacher Association (PTA), the Young Women's Christian Association (YWCA), the League of Women Voters, United Church Women, Women's International League for Peace and Freedom, the American Baptist Foreign Mission Society, the Human Rights Commission of the Baptist World Alliance, and related executive committee responsibilities required creative thinking and responsible program planning. The application of anthropological insights to public affairs issues and social concerns in community organizational work had become very important to me. So, although I had completed all my course requirements, the opportunity to study "Anthropology of Education" and "Anthropology of Development" under Philleo Nash again captured my enthusiastic attention.

To study with Dr. Nash was to be perpetually involved in an anthropological workshop. Using our intellectual tool kit, we were ever pondering the broad scope of the nature of human civilization. We were exploring the place of educational mechanisms in the development and maintenance of a societal structure that could foster and support personal freedom and political independence which are the natural privileges of human beings. Such is the birthright of every earthling.

We used our intellectual "tool kit" to help in our understanding of socioeconomic adaptation to restrictive environments, and the socioeconomic spatial niche which different minority populations (ethnic groupings) share in urbanizing America (i.e., United States of America). We thought of the role of the belief system as a "survival kit."

We talked about ecology as balance and interdependence in nature and about *ecosystem* as the community of human beings plus nature or "biology catching up with the social scientists." We learned the value of multimedia aids in teaching and to explore skills and techniques for adapting a variety of media materials for classroom teaching and at various levels in public education and for different learning experiences for community education for specific programs and projects. We deduced that education, being a cultural process, could be used to *close* rather than *perpetuate* the gap between expectation and reality, in projects and programs for the general welfare and the overall quality of life and human environmental concerns.

Dr. Nash believed in education as an instrument for the creation of new human values. He was concerned about the thought processes that followed culture contacts and culture conflicts. We were taught to observe different people and groups with different degrees of technological development; different levels of socioeconomic development, social control mechanisms, or governance patterns; and different religions. We learned to see how some contact groups entering the domain of a settled group to *learn,* soon begin *teaching.* Ere long the spontaneity in a contact situation gives way to coercion, indoctrination, and manipulation. As discontinuities follow rapid social change, education must be employed as an instrument for the creation of new human values.

We became acquainted with the teaching of Robert Redfield, for whom education was identified with the process of "cultural transmission and renewal," which is present in all societies and is the process by which societies persist and change.

Dr. Nash believed, with Bronislaw Malinowski, that "culture is an organic unit" and recognized the dangers of "tampering" with any aspect of traditional culture lest unforeseeable consequences occur.

All the above-mentioned teachings and insights communicated to me had great meaning for me as I pursued my research on Carlisle Indian School and Native American education for my dissertation. However, his teachings had an even greater impact on me in my volunteering with the American Baptist Foreign Mission Society and my teaching of prospective missionaries at the School of Theology at Virginia Union University, Richmond, Virginia. When missionaries come home on furlough after several years in the field, it is the custom of the foreign mission society to hold "re-entry retreats" at a conference center for the missionaries and their families prior to the missionaries' being sent out on deputation assignments. How does the sensitive, enlightened missionary report to an ordinary church congregation on the theological issue of baptism and church membership in a polygamous society when the missionary can see that the family ethic of that social structure precludes the possibility of the existence of any widows or any orphans, and the widows become their deceased husband's brother's additional wives? How can the conscientious mission executive become enlightened enough to help missionaries avoid feeling guilt-ridden by not being completely truthful with very conservative churches and very evangelical church members?

Fortunately, theological education is now addressing such problems—mainly because of the influence of linguistic anthropologists who have been engaged in biblical translation work worldwide.

My Carlisle Indian School dissertation was recently used in government hearings in Albuquerque, New Mexico, by former Indian Commissioner Robert L. Bennett. I asked Dr. Bennett, now retired, to comment on the influence of Philleo Nash in his life and service with the Bureau of Indian Affairs and *now* as consultant on American Indians.

I share with you his response, dated April 11, 1988:

> It is an honor for me to write you about Philleo Nash with whom I became acquainted while attending various meetings and conferences relating to Indian affairs. I was always impressed with his knowledge, insights and the special concerns he had for Indian people. Being a tribal member myself, this was especially appealing to me.

After the election of President John F. Kennedy, there was a vacancy in the position of Commissioner of Indian Affairs. It was my good fortune to chair a meeting of national Indian leaders for the purpose of recommending someone to be appointed to the position. The result was the unanimous recommendation of Philleo Nash to the administration that he be appointed Commissioner of Indian Affairs. As you know, based upon a special statute adopted in the early 1800s, the appointment of that office is a presidential appointment subject to consent of the United States Senate. We felt fortunate that Philleo was subsequently appointed and confirmed.

Philleo inherited a difficult situation because of the national policy of termination of Indian tribes and a bureaucracy which had been working under this policy for some time. It did not take Philleo long to turn this around and create within the Bureau of Indian Affairs a sensitivity to the needs of the Indian people and to provide leadership in developing programs to alleviate these needs. He also was very effective in getting other federal and state agencies interested in the plight of the American Indians. In doing this, he also created a congenial working relationship between the Indian tribes and the Bureau of Indian Affairs which was one of suspicion and mistrust.

It was my good fortune to succeed Philleo as Commissioner of Indian Affairs and my task was made much easier by the wonderful work he had done as my predecessor. I considered it the highlight of my career to have worked under his leadership and supervision and this experience stood me in good stead as his successor. I will never forget him or what he did by his administration to prepare me for the position. To him, I will always be grateful.

Education is a cultural process. Anthropology is a humanizing science. It held a quintessential place in the teachings and lifestyle of Philleo Nash.

Philleo Nash and Georgetown Day School

Edith Rosenfels Nash

In talking about Philleo's work in starting Georgetown Day School, I have a hard time separating what he did and thought from what I did and thought. We did so much of it together, and for so long, that I seem to be talking about us as a pair as though we were one person. However, I am trying to focus on him at a distance and a little background may help—how it came to be that two anthropologists got involved in schooling.

Philleo and I met at the University of Chicago anthropology department, and our introduction to cultural anthropology was largely joint. Before that Philleo had studied at the University of Wisconsin as an undergraduate—first in Meiklejohn's Experimental College, and then in the anthropology department with Ralph Linton and Charlotte Gower. For many years he rejected Meiklejohn, but eventually he overcame his resistance and acknowledged its importance in his intellectual development.

Philleo's description of his life at Meiklejohn's College is contained in a quote from an article he wrote for the spring 1986 issue of *Voices of Youth,* a publication of the Meiklejohn Education Foundation (1986b). He wrote:

> When the Experimental College opened its doors in 1927 I was among the first 120 young men who signed up. But I became a malcontent, received average grades or worse, concentrated on music and languages outside the College and dropped out for a semester as soon as the two years were over.
>
> Today, fifty-nine years later, I am an enthusiastic Board Member who voted to keep alive the Experimental College name and idea when we formed the Meiklejohn Education Foundation. What happened in between? In the process of educating others I became educated.
>
> An essential component of the Experimental College design was the comparative study of cultures, with the educational objective of examining social problems and their solutions. The comparison of cultures with scientific objectives is the subject matter of cultural anthropology. This much of the Experimental College rubbed off on me and when I returned to the university after three months respite waiting on tables in California, I signed up with the then new major in anthropology. Other opportunities lacking during the depression, I went on to graduate school and a Ph.D. in anthropology. I ended up as a professor in Canada.
>
> . . . By the time the war ended in 1945 I had two children of my own who were ready for school. Washington, D.C., still had racially segregated schools and four years of war had eroded even that unequal school system. To give our children a good, democratic education my wife Edith and I, with others, started our own school.

Philleo continued:

> Then the lessons of the Experimental College really began to come home. Our self-designed school had to be cooperatively organized and operated; it had to be built on respect for individuals and their cultures, and so it had to be truly integrated as to students, parents, staff and Board; and it had to be based on the belief that learning is a delight but that it is hard work.
>
> We began with only five families and seven children, but we grew quickly. I was president of the Board for the first few years until my daughters outgrew the school and I

had to step down, since Board members were elected from among the parent body. My wife was active in the school from the beginning and was director for fifteen years after 1960.

Today it is a large institution with nearly a thousand students and a faculty of more than a hundred. It is still integrated in fact, not in theory. Many changes have been made in the educational design, but it is substantially the same school and it has stood up against all the winds of change that have swept through the nation's capital in the past forty years.

A little more background—how we grew up in anthropology at the University of Chicago:

We took Radcliffe-Brown's introductory course together. My notebook has notes on the lectures on the right-hand page, and notes to and from Philleo on the left-hand side. "Does he really wear corsets?" and other impertinent comments. Philleo became Radcliffe-Brown's research assistant and was able to pay his bills at the Chinese restaurant and the local bar we went to, and learned to make a "silver shadow," Radcliffe-Brown's major contribution to cocktail time.

I had one year of graduate work in anthropology at Chicago and a field trip to Tularosa, New Mexico, working with informants on the Mescalero Reservation under Morris Opler's careful tutelage. Philleo came to visit on his way west to start his research on Klamath Reservation on a predoctoral fellowship and we arranged to get married, which we did in 1935. Back at Klamath I learned to cook on a wood stove and Philleo did the research, both with documents and with informants, which shook down into his doctoral thesis on "The Place of Religious Revivalism in the Formation of the Intercultural Community on the Klamath Reservation" published in Fred Eggan's volume *Social Anthropology of North American Tribes*.

Two social scientists besides Radcliffe-Brown who were important to Philleo were Robert Redfield and Harold Lasswell. Philleo and Harold Lasswell became close friends in the summer of 1935 when Harold was teaching at California and Philleo was doing the preparatory work in Berkeley on Klamath, mostly with Cora du Bois. Philleo's view of nativistic movements and his method of analyzing them— an important part of his worldview all his life—was formed during this time and was the underpinning of his subsequent work in solving problems in government at many levels.

Philleo's first academic job was at the University of Toronto where we lived for four years. Both our children were born there and became our major joint concern. Philleo enjoyed teaching at Toronto and doing archeology for the Royal Ontario Museum, but the atmosphere of the university and museum—rigid, anti-American, hidebound—combined with the low salary (Philleo made $1800 a year when he went to Toronto, and after four years of hard work, he was offered $2200) and the absence of civil liberties after Canada entered the war in the fall of 1939, finally made him eager to return to the United States. He was very aware of Edward Sapir's long isolation in Ottawa and its devastating effect, and was eager to avoid a similar isolation. These were the days of Toronto's blue laws—the only place to buy the New York Times on Sunday was a speakeasy.

We returned to Wisconsin Rapids, and Philleo became the manager of the family cranberry business. He worked under his father's direction, organized the Indian camp, did some archeology at Du Bay, and taught once a week at the University of Wisconsin in Madison. I longed for life in the mainstream, as Philleo's mother had always done, and after Pearl Harbor our escape hatch opened up.

Harold Lasswell was staffing a Groups and Organizations component of the Office of Facts and Figures that Archibald MacLeish headed. Roosevelt was president and "Dr. Win the War" had replaced "Dr. New Deal" in Roosevelt's words. Social scientists were flocking to Washington, and we saw a lot of them. Most all my energy was taken up with moving, housing, and caring for young daughters and finding out that the mainstream did not sweep my problems away.

Philleo noticed that the social scientists did not study the bureaucracy as they had studied their previous research subjects. He was fascinated by how government works, and spent a lot of time finding out where he might be needed and for what. The big shots in social science who came through thought that the bureaucrats would ask them how to proceed in making policy and were baffled when they did not. Some learned slowly how to be useful. Later on, I worked for Ruth Benedict in the Office of War Information, Bureau of Overseas Intelligence, and by then she had learned where her memos went after she wrote them, and what she had to do to get them read.

From the Office of Facts and Figures Philleo went to the Office of War Information-Domestic Branch (Elmer Davis was in charge) and with a black newspaperman, Ted Poston, began to keep track of episodes of race tension, as it might affect production in war plants. This led them into association with Jonathan Daniels at the White House, interested in liaison with black groups, and methods of analyzing racial tensions and preventing outbreaks that could impede production of essential materials. The War Powers Act gave the White House the ability to radically address grievances of black workers and prevent interruptions. Several episodes were prevented from escalating into major work stoppages. Thurgood Marshall once said to Philleo, "If you'd been at Lincoln's side there never would have been a Civil War . . . (and we'd all still be slaves)."

Philleo was very much involved in applying social science techniques—to keep track of rumors, to measure racial confrontations, and to monitor the black press. *To make something happen* was heady stuff, quite different from life in the academy, and when he moved over to the White House office in Old State, he had a very good telephone number from which to collect information. Truman inherited him from Roosevelt and wanted him to stay on, much to Philleo's initial surprise, and Philleo stayed for the duration as one of the assistants with a "passion for anonymity," a charge laid upon them by FDR. Philleo always said President Truman was the best boss he ever had. His work was largely with black groups and organizations and also with the president, in integrating the armed forces, writing Truman's speeches (a famous one at Howard University, and another in Brooks Square, Harlem in the 1948 election—the one Truman won) helping create the President's Commission on Civil Rights and guiding their report. Some of this work is summarized in Philleo's recent article in *Human Organization,* "Science, Politics, and Human Values: A Memoir" (1986a). This article was the basis of Philleo's speech at the Reno meeting of the Society for Applied Anthropology in April 1986 when Philleo received the Malinowski Award.

In the fall of 1944 we met Agnes Inglis, later Agnes Inglis O'Neil, at the King-Smith school across the street from our apartment on Swann Street near Dupont Circle in Washington. Our older daughter, Maggie, had started public school, a sorry excuse for schooling, in our neighborhood. It was a segregated school; many teachers were new substitutes and hysterical as well as incompetent; and besides, she hated to go. Our younger daughter, Sally, was enrolled in a little nursery school, not harmful, but uneventful and dreary.

Aggie, as she was known to everyone, was just starting a school across the street. I went over to visit; a friend from the University of Chicago had phoned to let us know of the school's existence. Two dancers, Ethel Butler and David Campbell, were helping get the room ready—washing a fish bowl for the opening day. Aggie had found a circular staircase behind the room which was to be used for the children and put the name of each child expected on a step. They were all so warm and welcoming, so cued in to children's minds and bodies. I felt I must have Maggie's name on one of those steps; Aggie put it there. So Maggie came, and Sally soon after. Our girls were two out of seven children in that first class—a variety of ages and temperaments, and one of them was black. Everything proceeded naturally and the children learned and grew. There was a small room adjoining where the Loose Tooth Study Club met and read out of real books. "Reading readiness" was determined by whether you had a loose tooth—as good a way as any. Later in the year, Ag gathered the parents together and a committee was formed. Philleo became chairman and took on finding a place to hold school since the King-Smiths were about to terminate the day school. The art, dance, and drama teachers who had taught for the King-Smiths in the evenings and in the Day School during the day continued with us and were very instrumental in the educational process under Aggie's direction. From the beginning, the arts were central to the school's program. Both our daughters are dancers today, with a strong interest in ritual.

Social studies were also important. As Philleo wrote in a Georgetown Day School newsletter written in 1971:

> GDS set out to be appropriate to its position in the nation's capital; to be integrated when segregation was the rule; to be available to the representatives of the new countries who were baffled by the ambivalence of the area schooling; to contribute to the educational cross-currents of the public and other private schools; to stay downtown when other private schools were moving to the suburbs. These policies require observation and analysis of the social life of which our school is a part, together with decisions as to the right way to go. This is the stuff of which social studies are made: part science, part ethics, close to the people.
>
> This is why social studies in the various grade levels of GDS—from the lowest grades all the way through to the high school—are centered around understanding the cultural stream in which we live. A distant part of that stream is the early evolution of man himself. Less distant are the great river valley civilizations of the ancient world—Nile, Euphrates, Indus and Yellow. Less familiar, but of great importance are the city-state cultures of the New World, destroyed even to their written records by racial and religious intolerance. We do not omit the rise of the nation-states of Western Europe which have given birth to our own institutions of law and government either by incorporation or rebellion. And in the world of here-and-now characterized by much expression of dissatisfaction through direct action; where the liberal philosophy of togetherness seems rejected daily in favor of ethnic separateness, surely it is of paramount importance that we should develop knowledge and awareness of how we Americans came together to become what we are—and what we would like to be but are not.

Philleo's article continues:

> A generation ago we could have taught the permanence of institutions and the beauties of the democratic process. Today the denial of these values reaches into our own families as older siblings get to know the meaning of "bail" and younger siblings find out for themselves that pride in race and culture are real when the melting pot is hot. In many parts of the world the democratic process has not survived or does not appeal. In such a world it is not enough to assert that democracy is good. It must be lived through and made to be good, in our time and place.

That is why, in GDS, individual teachers are encouraged to create courses in social studies that, within the general framework of culture history, relate to the people and their life-styles around us. Such a curriculum will vary from year to year, teacher to teacher, course to course. Yet it will be steady because it is based on interpretation of the long-developing world culture of which we are a part and which is a part of us. It is not "history" but it makes use of history; it is not "geography" but it makes use of geography. It is neither "progressive" nor "traditional." It is intended to develop the students' powers of observation and interpretation and to make them aware that their own lives reflect the lives of all others around them, especially those that are very close in the GDS community.

I would not like to leave the impression that Philleo and I always agreed about issues of daily life at Georgetown Day School. When I became director in 1961 after a stormy division into warring camps of the parent body, I felt I had to take account of all constituencies and work with all parents who still had children in the school. Philleo's greater political experience led him to advise my sticking with my supporters, promoting their election to the Board and making few concessions to those who had not supported me. Of course, it was resolved by events. The parents who had been the enemy either left the school or got used to me.

Later on, Philleo supported the Board of Trustees when they wanted me to mind. He had been Board Chairman during the crucial first years of the school, and he felt the conflict between the board and me was not based on any educational issues but rather a competition as to "who speaks for the school" and that I was over-eager to do the speaking. I was sure that real issues were involved: some parents wanted the school to be more rigidly structured, wanted a guarantee from the school that their children would get into Harvard (even when we stopped at junior high at that time). They wanted teachers to have more degrees and for the building to be cleaner. They wanted to have a gym and a more standard athletic program including showers, to prohibit dogs in school, and to stop kids from calling teachers by first names. They wanted the classroom atmosphere to be more competitive (if the child they were concerned with was fast) or less competitive (if the child they were concerned with was slow).

I felt my role was to preserve the school's value system, encourage learning at many levels and promote high academic standards (devoting some energy to see that everybody was given an opportunity to achieve), respect some disorder in the service of learning, open doors for children and not attempt to march them through them. After a while Philleo realized that a small but determined segment of the board was eager to ease me out of the directorship and he stopped trying to get me to submit to higher authority. He comforted me instead, telling me about all the jobs he had been fired from. At parent meetings he identified himself as the director-consort.

About qualifications: teachers were chosen for their enthusiasm for their subject, or the age group they were teaching and their ability to relate to students and to learn any material needed. And about dogs: I liked to have dogs in school and other animals as well. Nothing impressed visitors and new students as much as the sight of a dog or two in the hall. Aggie had bred poodles and often brought a whole litter to school. One day a chimpanzee visited and drank a box of milk with a straw in the kindergarten, a real tool-user. Children, in elementary grades especially, identify and frolic with animals in school, take care of them and sense their own nearness to the animal world.

Festivals and celebrations were important at Georgetown Day School, because Philleo thought they were important. In the spring of 1946 we were still at G Place, and a six-year-old boy named Nickie came to me and said, "I want to have a party for our Jews." That seemed like a good idea. I was Aggie's assistant at that time, in charge of parties and pencils. Nickie had been to his first-ever Seder the night before and was eager to spread the word. He said his mother would come to the school after work and bring matzoh and grape juice, which she did, and Nickie stood at the entrance of the big room and told each child to wash his hands.

I had been to only one Seder in my whole life, at age 10, and no one in our family practiced any Jewish rituals. It was 1945. Although World War II was just over, and Hitler had raised the consciousness of Jews as nothing else had ever done, the general secularization of all American culture had taken its toll with most of our Jewish parents and no one talked about religious observance in school. We were all atheists or agnostics or maybe Unitarians at school, along with being color-blind.

Of course, this didn't apply to Aggie, wayward daughter of a Presbyterian minister, who always read Scripture at Christmas and taught the children to understand the story of the birth of Jesus. She also wrote a play for the children about a miracle on Christmas Eve, when the animals in the stable talked at midnight and regretted their inability to plan. Aggie was raised in government in the New Deal, where planning was king.

So I helped Nickie stage our first Seder. I got Dante Radice, a very lapsed Episcopalian choir boy and our in-house storyteller, to tell the story of the Passover to the youngest children so they would have some idea what was coming off. We were all equally ignorant of the succession of events. Dante got up to Moses in the bulrushes before I came to get the children, but we knew it had to do with slavery and freedom and deliverance and the preservation of ancient values from long, long ago.

So after that, Passover became our spring festival. It was as solidified into the festival year as a Christian Christmas. Philleo felt it was important to preserve real meaning in festivals, not allowing them to drift into meaningless school programs. Later on, when I was director, many Jewish parents came to thank me and other people in the warm office for introducing their children to the Seder, long neglected in their homes. A black parent, not too familiar with matzoh balls at the big Seder lunch, came to say that once I mentioned the march from Selma to Montgomery, he knew it was his festival too.

One time at a parent's meeting when Philleo was chairman, he was asked, "Why does the school have all this religious stuff? We're nonbelievers and what do you have for us?" "For you," Philleo said, "we have Halloween."

And Halloween became, and still is, the children's holiday par excellence. We had parties, prizes, and a Halloween parade. Most made their own costumes and one could impersonate whoever one wanted. One time Shari Belafonte came as Harry Belafonte. One boy put a hollowed pumpkin over his head and came as a pumpkin. In the era of Twiggy, the British model, one boy came as Twiggy.

And we celebrated Japanese kite day on a windy day in spring. The children used to design and build their own kites and parents came to help. Martin Luther King's birthday was added with friends and associates of Dr. King's coming to share their memories with groups of students. In the high school, I remember an international food bazaar with the language classes preparing their national foods, and the lower school built a giant dragon for Chinese New Year. There was an African first fruits festival in first grade one year, and some other special celebrations came and went as students and teachers invented them.

In the early days, Philleo came to play the guitar and sing folk songs with the children, usually on Friday morning when he had to visit Grasslands, our next school location after G Place, to bleed the radiators in the antique heating system. He was on President Truman's White House staff by then, and after discussing the whole design of the school with the president—its multiracial character and do-it-yourself philosophy—the president told him whatever time he had to give to the school and be away from the White House was okay with him. We sang Burl Ives songs, John Jacob Niles songs, Woody Guthrie songs, and many of the mountain folk songs in the Cecil Sharp collection. Philleo invited Alan Lomax to sing at one of our early money-raising events, and Pete Seeger came to sing with the students when his brother Mike was a student.

Philleo was in charge of financial management (never Aggie's long suit), held board meetings at least once a week, negotiated for space and facilities, presided at parent meetings, raised some money from foundations, and left the education of the children to Aggie and her capable staff. The other parent board members were extremely helpful and dedicated to the success of Aggie's kind of teaching and the fledgling school.

Philleo wrote the bylaws with Carol Agger Fortas's help and could never understand how parents in subsequent years interpreted a parent-owned school as a parent-run school, since he had so clearly outlined the board's mission. The board was elected from the parent body. They chose the director. The director hired the teachers, admitted the students, and conducted the educational program. The parents were admitted to the corporation when a child was admitted and paid $10 for a share of stock (now called a membership). When the last child in a family was withdrawn, the parents were no longer members of the corporation and could get their $10 back if they wished. This made a circular design that pleased Philleo's sense of order and the flow of authority. It worked well while he was chairman and Aggie was director. Philleo had complete confidence in Ag's ability to know children and to build an environment in which all kinds could prosper. She came to depend on Philleo, happy to be relieved of financial management. Besides, they trusted each other.

I always felt that if we had made mistakes in raising our own children, Aggie and the school could rectify them. Our children's surviving grandparents lived at a distance and most parents in wartime Washington were far from home and any older generation's guidance or support. Our generation had mostly rejected the advice and example of our parents, this rebelliousness having come home to roost when we had children of our own. So we basked in Aggie's unqualified acceptance of us and our children.

Philleo often said the good parts of the educational system were kindergarten and graduate school—in between being rather a wasteland. He was eager to find materials that would introduce meaningful material into the school and about 1970 the marvelous course, "Man: A Course of Study," was published. It consisted of many pamphlets, films, and a projector even adults could operate, a course outline recommended for fifth grade, and the best introduction to human biology, the study of culture, and psychology for children ever put together. It did not correspond to the educationist's view of how fifth graders are or should be taught and resistance to it was enormous, although it was widely used in many classrooms across the country at a certain period. It even came to the attention of the Congress, which threatened to cut off appropriations to the National Science Foundation, which had supported it. Margaret Mead testified for it before the Congress but felt her task would have been easier if the component about an Eskimo group putting old people out on the ice to die had been omitted. Philleo and I read the whole course through and thought it was wonderful. We started in fourth grade where we had a course in prehistory already in place, and turned to the education of teachers to use the material.

There was a training course nearby developed at the Educational Development Center, which published the course, and five of our teachers were needled into attending. It was a hands-on course (one teacher learned how to dissect a salmon), but it was not an anthropology course, and our teachers felt they needed that. So Philleo came to GDS and gave a course called "Anthropology for Teachers." We invited teachers from other schools and it increased the use of the "Man: A Course of Study" materials, not only in fourth grade but in the seventh grade and in the new high school. Philleo had the teachers prepare lesson plans for social science projects in any class from kindergarten through high school, and I observed that it changed their view of many cultural and biological materials. He also showed how to use film, how to take notes in the dark, and other practical considerations. Philleo was in the anthropology department of American University by this time and continued his course, "Anthropology for Teachers," there.

The new high school curriculum was planned in 1969–70. Philleo chaired the social science component, and two courses in anthropology resulted—a beginning course utilizing the Anthropology Curriculum Study Project from Chicago that Macmillan had just published, and several book and film combinations such as Truffaut's L'Enfant Sauvage teamed with The Wild Boy of Aveyron, about Professor Jean-Marc Itard's work with the boy who had lived without human contact. This course was taught at the high school by Philleo and Joe Ferber, a high school teacher, who continued it for several years. A second course on the American Indian was introduced. We hear from various adults who have gone into applied anthropology fields—one in law in Alaska, one in film at the Smithsonian—as a result of this stimulus in high school. Some study of cultures and use of multicultural materials has leaked into other courses, into history courses primarily. There is even now a course called "Human Behavior" taught in the high school. This course developed from one published by the Educational Development Center, the same organization that developed "Man: A Course of Study."

Margaret Mead was very generous in giving time to Georgetown Day School. Philleo got her to come to our 25th and again to our 30th anniversary celebrations in 1970 and 1975. She stayed with us overnight in our apartment, telephoning all over the world in the early morning telling friends and colleagues what they should be doing. After a long day at school, talking to groups of students and teachers, showing films, rushing home for dinner, and back for an evening lecture, I sacked out as soon as we hit home. Several hours later I awoke and tottered out to the living room where Philleo and Margaret were still at it. Margaret had her notebook open and was saying, "Now, Philleo, what's all this about treaties?" Philleo was lecturing on the history of Indian-white relations in the United States.

"Taking Note" was a perfect title for the Odyssey program Ann Peck produced for PBS about Margaret Mead. We both participated in the program along with many others, and were very pleased with the results. Philleo also helped Jane Howard get started on her biography of Margaret. She cordially acknowledged his help.

When Margaret came to Georgetown Day School for one of the anniversaries, she compared GDS and Downtown Community School in New York which started about the same time. Her daughter, Cathy Bateson, attended Downtown Community for a time. Margaret reminisced about meeting with us in the kitchen of our apartment on Swann Street about 1945 when Georgetown Day School as a parent corporation was planned. She said if I ever wrote the school's history, she would cooperate and maybe we would discover why Georgetown Day succeeded when Downtown Community failed.

Philleo was always available during the time I was director of GDS. During the Six-Day War, our miniature Rambos in the fifth grade, just across from the office, cheered and hooted at Israeli victories when they came in the morning. I asked Philleo to come to school and talk to the students, and he did. He gave a short history of Palestine, the movement of peoples beginning with prehistoric times, the recognition of Israel in the Truman Administration—with which he had been very involved—and a little about the family of languages and culture common to both sides in that war. The children were goggled-eyed. "I never knew any of that!" the energetic Jewish partisans screeched as they left the room. "Nobody ever told me that!"

At a memorial service for Philleo at GDS, held a few weeks after his death on October 12, 1987, one black man, a former student at Georgetown Day, testified that he had felt very comfortable there, but never knew why it was so different from the world he encountered later, in school and in adult life. During the memorial occasion, he realized the school had been a singular experience for him of un-racism, which he now could attribute to the school's having been started by an anthropologist. He never heard anything about "anthropology" when he was a student at Georgetown Day School. But it made a difference, nonetheless.

References Cited

Lurie, Nancy Oestreich
    1961   The Voice of the American Indian: A Report on the American Indian Chicago Conference. Current Anthropology 2(5):478–500.
    1972   Two Dollars. *In* Crossing Cultural Boundaries. Solon T. Kimball and James B. Watson, eds. Pp. 151–163. San Francisco: Chandler Publishing Co.
McNett, Charles W., Jr.
    1988   Anthropology. *In* Encyclopaedia Britannica Yearbook of Science and the Future 1988. Pp. 275–278. Chicago: Encyclopaedia Britannica.
Miller, Helen Miner, and Nancy Oestreich Lurie
    1963   Report on Wisconsin Winnebago Project: Contribution of Community Development to the Prevention of Dependency. Vol. 1. Washington, D.C.: HEW, U.S. Social Security Administration.
Morrissey, Charles T.
    1966   Interview with Philleo Nash held on March 8, 1966; typescript in the John F. Kennedy Library.
Nash, Philleo
    1937   The Place of Religious Revivalism in the Formation of the Intercultural Community on the Klamath Reservation. *In* The Social Anthropology of North American Tribes; Essays in Social Organization, Law and Religion. Fred Eggan, ed. Pp. 377–442. Chicago: University of Chicago Press.
    1947   Final Report, Fair Employment Practice Committee, June 28, 1946. Washington, D.C.: U.S. Government Printing Office.
    1970   Applied Anthropology and the Concept of Guided Acculturation. Paper delivered at the annual meeting of the American Anthropological Association, San Diego.
    1986a   Science, Politics and Human Values: A Memoir. Human Organization 45(3):189–201.
    1986b   Fifty-Nine Years of the Ex-College. Voices of Youth, Spring. Sonoma, Calif.: Meiklejohn Education Foundation, Educational Goals Study Group.
Sieber, Nadine Day, and Nancy Oestreich Lurie
    1965   Report on Wisconsin Winnebago Project: Contribution of Community Development to the Prevention of Dependency. Volume 2. Washington, D.C.: HEW, U.S. Social Security Administration.

About the Authors

Ada Deer is Professor of Indian Studies at the University of Wisconsin. Her acquaintance with Philleo Nash began during his term as Commissioner of Indian Affairs. They shared a commitment to American Indians and to the political scene, and, like Philleo, she has run for elective office in Wisconsin.

Fred Eggan was an Instructor and fellow graduate student at the University of Chicago, and shared a lifelong interest in American Indian communities with Philleo. He is Distinguished Professor Emeritus at the University of Chicago, now living in Sante Fe, and is associated there with the Laboratory of Anthropology.

Katherine Spencer Halpern is Professor Emeritus at American University, and had known Philleo since her student days at the University of Chicago. She has worked as an applied anthropologist in a number of American Indian communities. She too now lives in Santa Fe, and is associated with the Wheelwright Museum.

Ruth Landman is a Professor at American University, and began her acquaintance with Philleo Nash when she invited him to join the anthropology department there. Together they later organized a Margaret Mead Institute, and served as officers of the Anthropological Society of Washington.

Nancy Oestreich Lurie is Head Curator of Anthropology at the Milwaukee Public Museum. Her special connection with Philleo was forged through their shared concern and work for the Wisconsin Winnebago. She lists herself as an action anthropologist, an orientation that made them good allies in such a cause.

Pearl Walker-McNeil is Professor Emeritus of Ecumenical Christianity at Virginia Theological Seminary. She was one of Philleo Nash's doctoral students, and wrote her dissertation on the Carlisle Indian School's aggressively acculturative program. In her reminiscence she shows how she has integrated her applied anthropology into her life of action with an ecumenical Christian career.

Edith Rosenfels Nash shared Philleo's life as wife, fellow anthropologist and fellow educator through more than fifty years, and now carries on as successor in the cranberry business. They first met as anthropology students at the University of Chicago.

James Officer served as Associate Commissioner of Indian Affairs while Philleo Nash was Commissioner. He is now Professor of Anthropology at the University of Arizona, where his work continues to concern itself with Indians as well as with Mexican-Americans.

Appendix 1: Archival Materials

Several sources of information are available to anyone who wishes to study the ways in which Philleo Nash carried out his work as an applied anthropologist. His professional papers are housed in the Presidential Library of President Harry S. Truman in Independence, Missouri. They have been catalogued and organized by Archivist Philip Lagerquist. The personal archives of Philleo Nash cover his work on minority affairs, race tension, civil rights legislation, the Fair Employment Practices Commission, and other matters during his years on the president's staff; later boxes cover the years in Wisconsin politics and twenty boxes concern the years as Commissioner of Indian Affairs. There are memos, drafts of speeches for the president, correspondence and notes to the files, as well as clippings from then current publications relevant to topics under consideration. The library also has the archival materials of David Niles, under whom Philleo worked for a good part of the Truman years. These papers are all open for inspection. A further archival resource is available at the University of Arizona, in the Stewart Udall Archives.

Secondly, there are two sets of sound tapes. An interview was conducted by Drs. Bernice Kaplan and Kathryn Molohan during the 1982 annual meetings of the Society for Applied Anthropology as part of a project to gather oral history materials on the history of applied anthropology. Dr. Molohon, at Laurentian University, and Dr. Van Kemper, of Southern Methodist University, have copies of this interview, which is about two hours long. The tape concentrates on the years between 1941 and the early 1950s. Tapes of an earlier interview can be found in the John F. Kennedy Memorial Library in Boston; this one deals with Philleo Nash's entire service in the federal government.

Appendix 2

This list of activities and writings is based upon a Curriculum Vitae that Philleo Nash prepared early in 1987.

Curriculum Vitae and Bibliography

Personal

Born: Wisconsin Rapids, October 25, 1909
Educated: Wisconsin Rapids Public Schools; University of Wisconsin Madison (A.B., 1932); University of Chicago (Ph.D., 1937)
Family: Married Edith Rosenfels, Oak Park, IL, November 2, 1935; children: Maggie (Mrs. E. C. Kast) and Sally

Honors

Faculty Award, University of Wisconsin, Green Bay	1973
Distinguished Service Award, American Anthropological Association	1984
Bronislaw Malinowski Award, Society for Applied Anthropology	1986

Academic Appointments

Lecturer in Anthropology, University of Toronto, and Assistant Keeper, Ethnological Collections, Royal Ontario Museum, Toronto	1937–41
Special Lecturer, University of Wisconsin, Madison	1941–42
Adjunct Professor of Anthropology, American University	1971–73
Professor of Anthropology, American University and Faculty, University Learning Center, American University	1973–77
Director, University Learning Center, American University	1976–77
Professor Emeritus, Anthropology, American University	1977–87
Director, Special Symposium: "The Legacy of Margaret Mead," American University	March 1980
Meiklejohn Fellow in Residence, University of Wisconsin Madison	April 1984

Government

Special Assistant, Office of War Information	1942–46
Special Consultant to the Secretary of War	1943
Special Assistant, The White House	1946–52
Administrative Assistant to the President, USA	1952–53
Lieutenant Governor of Wisconsin	1959–61
U.S. Commissioner of Indian Affairs	1961–66
American Specialist Program (India), U.S. Department of State	1966

Anthropological Societies

Treasurer, American Anthropological Association	1968–70
President, Society for Applied Anthropology	1970–71

| Secretary, Section H (Anthropology), American Association for the Advancement of Science | 1974–78 |
| President, Anthropological Society of Washington | 1975–76 |

Public Service

President, Georgetown Day School, Washington, D.C.	1945–52
Chairman, Wisconsin Democratic Party	1955–57
Vice-Chairman, Menominee Voting Trust	1959
Chairman, Wisconsin Refugee Year	1961
Member, Board of Directors, Meiklejohn Education Foundation	1982–87
Member, Board of Trustees, Institute for Intercultural Studies (Margaret Mead, Founder)	1970–82
Member, Advisory Council, Institute for Intercultural Studies	1982–87

Business

Vice-President, Biron Cranberry Co., Inc., Wisconsin Rapids	1930–46
President, Biron Cranberry Co., Inc.	1946–77
President, Wisconsin Cranberry Growers Association	1959–60
President and Manager, Biron Cranberry Co., Inc.	1977–87

Bibliography

I. *Scholarly Publications*

1933   The Excavation of Ross Mound Group I. Bulletin, Milwaukee Public Museum 16(1). 46 pp.

1937   The Place of Religious Revivalism in the Formation of the Intercultural Community of Klamath Reservation. *In* Social Anthropology of North American Tribes: Essays in Social Organization, Law, and Religion. Fred Eggan, ed. Pp. 377–442. Chicago: University of Chicago Press.

1943   An Introduction to the Problem of Race Tension. *In* The North American Indian Today. C. T. Loram and T. F. McIlwraith, eds. Pp. 331–335. Toronto: University of Toronto Press.

1955   Progress in Race Relations. Fiftieth Anniversary Address, Abraham Lincoln Centre, Chicago. Unity 141(1):12–13.

1962   Indian Administration in the United States. Lecture, University of Toronto. Vital Speeches 1963.

1964   American Indian Affairs Today. Address to City Club of Portland, Portland, OR, (also U.S. Department of Interior [USDI] litho, 10pp., July 26). The Delphian Quarterly 47(2):4–10, 34.

1967   Research in American Indian Education. Proceedings of the National Research Conference on American Indian Education, Society for the Study of Social Problems, Pennsylvania State University. Pp. 6–30.

1968   *Review of* The Klamath Tribe: A People and their Reservation by Theodore Stern. American Anthropologist 70(1):116–118.

1970   Whither Indian Education. School Review 79(1):99–108.

1973a   Applied Anthropology and the Concept of Guided Acculturation. The Indian Historian 6:23–35.

1973b   To Live on this Earth: A Review Article. Council on Anthropology and Education Newsletter 4(2):33–35.

1975   Education Policy. Discussion of remarks by Hon. Elliot Richardson. Proceedings, Anthropological Society of Washington, D.C.

1977   The Eskimo Films of Asen Balikci. American Anthropologist 79(2):510–512.

1979a   Anthropologist in the White House. Practicing Anthropology 1(3):3, 23, 24.

1979b   Foreword. *In* The Commissioners of Indian Affairs 1824–1977. Robert M. Kvasnicka and Herman J. Viola, eds. Pp. xiii–xiv. Lincoln: University of Nebraska Press.

1980   Philleo Nash. *In* The Truman White House: The Administration of the Presidency, 1945–53. Francis H. Heller, ed. Pp. 52–56. Lawrence: Regents Press of Kansas.

1983   Termination. *In* Indian Self-Rule: Fifty Years under the Indian Reorganization Act. Pp. 22–23. Sun Valley, ID: Institute of the American West.

1984   *Review of* Handbook of American Indian Law by Felix Cohen. American Anthropologist 86(1):183–184.

1986a   Science, Politics, and Human Values: A Memoir. Human Organization 45(3):189–201.

1986b   Fifty-Nine Years of the Ex-College. Voices of Youth, Spring. Sonoma, CA: Meiklejohn Education Foundation, Educational Goals Study Group.

1986c   Panelist: Indian Self-Rule: First-Hand Accounts of Indian-White Relations from Roosevelt to Reagan. Kenneth R. Philip, ed. Salt Lake City: Howe Brothers.

II. *Public Policy and World War II Information Publications* (Editor and Coauthor)

1944a   Leadership and the Negro Soldier. Army Service Forces Training Manual M5. U.S. Government Printing Office. 104 pp.

1944b   Spanish Speaking Americans in the War. Washington, D.C.: Office of the Coordinator of Inter-American Affairs. 16 pp.

1945   Enemy Japan. Office of War Information, U.S. Government Printing Office. 26 pp.

1947a   Final Report, Fair Employment Practice Committee, June 28, 1946. U.S. Government Printing Office. i–xvi + 28 pp.

1947b   To Secure These Rights, The Report of the President's Committee on Civil Rights. U.S. Government Printing Office. 178 pp.

1950   Freedom to Serve, President's Committee on Equality of Treatment and Opportunity in the Armed Services. U.S. Government Printing Office.

1961   Report to the Secretary of the Interior. Task Force on Indian Affairs, U.S. Dept. of Interior.

1962   Statement before the Interior Department Subcommittee of the House of Representatives Committee on Appropriations, relating to Indian Bureau program objectives.

1965a   Briefing on Indian Affairs. Subcommittee on Indian Affairs, Committee on Interior and Insular Affairs, U.S. House of Representatives, Committee Print. Pp. 75–116, January 27.

1965b   Report to the Senate Appropriations Committee on the Navajo Border-town Dormitory Program. USDI litho. 72 pp.

III. *Public Statements, Lectures, Addresses, and Interviews*

American Indian Affairs

1961a   Statement: Nomination for Commissioner of Indian Affairs. Hearings before the Committee of Interior and Insular Affairs, United States Senate, Eighty-seventh Congress, First Session, on the nomination of Philleo Nash to be Commissioner of Indian Affairs, August 14 and 17. Washington, D.C.: U.S. Government Printing Office (GPO).

1961b   Statement: Congressional Record. Commissioner of Indian Affairs. September 20. Pp. 19204–19210. Washington, D.C.: U.S. GPO.

1961c   Address: 18th Annual Convention, National Congress of American Indians, Lewiston, ID. USDI litho. 9 pp.

1961d   Remarks: Conference of Indian Bureau Superintendents, Denver, CO. USDI litho. 9 pp.

1962a   Statement: Interior Department and Related Agencies Subcommittee of the U.S. House of Representatives Appropriations Committee. USDI litho. 13 pp.

1962b   Remarks: Joint Meeting of the Pawnee, Ponca, Tonkawa, Kaw, and Otoe-Missouri Tribes of Oklahoma and the Potawatomi, Sac and Fox, Iowa and Kickapoo Tribes of Kansas at the Junior High School Auditorium, Ponca City, OK. USDI ditto. 4 pp.

1962c   Remarks: Meeting of the Osage Indian Tribe, Pawhuska, OK. USDI ditto. 4 pp.

1962d   Address: 3rd Annual Conference on Adult Education and Community Development, Arizona State University. USDI ditto, 8 pp.

1962e   Address: The New Trail for American Indians. 79th annual meeting of the Indian Rights Association, Philadelphia, unpublished MS. 11 pp.

1962f   Press Release: Excerpts from address before the Central States Anthropological Society, St. Louis, MO. USDI ditto. 2 pp.

1962g   Address: Annual Meeting of the Association of American Indian Affairs, New York. USDI litho. 7 pp.

1962h   Press Release: Excerpts from remarks before a meeting of the Wisconsin Associated Press Association, Wisconsin Rapids. USDI ditto. 4 pp.

1962i   Address: Commencement Exercises, Eastern Montana College of Education, Billings. USDI litho. 13 pp.

1962j   Remarks: Annual Omaha Powwow, Macy, NE. USDI ditto. 5 pp.

1962k   Address: 19th Annual Convention, National Congress of American Indians, Cherokee, NC. USDI ditto. 8 pp.

1962l   Remarks: Annual Meeting of the Governors' Interstate Indian Council, Phoenix. USDI litho. 3 pp.

1962m   Address: Indian Administration in the United States. School of Graduate Studies, University of Toronto. USDI litho. 11 pp.

1963a   Lecture: Conference of Bureau of Indian Affairs Area Directors of Education. USDI ditto. 24 pp.

1963b   Remarks: Meeting of the Army-Navy Chapter of the Daughters of the American Revolution, Washington, D.C. USDI ditto. 2 pp.

1963c   Remarks: Marlboro Student Forum, Marlboro College, Marlboro, VT. USDI ditto. 1 p.

1963d   Address: The Causes of Indian Poverty. University of Arizona Sunday Evening Forum, Tucson. USDI litho. 8 pp.

1963e   Remarks: Guided Acculturation: Indian Affairs Today. American Ortho-Psychiatric Association, Washington, D.C. USDI ditto. 3 pp.

1963f   Remarks: Executive Council, National Congress of American Indians, Washington, D.C. USDI litho. 5 pp.

1963g   Remarks: 4th Annual Conference on Adult Education and Indian Community Development, Tempe, AZ. USDI ditto. 5 pp.

1963h   Remarks: Inaugural Ceremonies, Chairman and Vice-Chairman, Navajo Tribal Council, Window Rock, AZ. USDI ditto. 1 p.

1963i   Remarks: Meeting of federal officials from Pennsylvania and Western New York to discuss the proposed national service program, Pittsburgh. USDI ditto. 2 pp.

1963j   Remarks: Annual Indian Breakfast of the National Society, Daughters of the American Revolution, Washington, D.C. USDI ditto. 2 pp.

1963k   Address: Arizona Commission of Indian Affairs, Phoenix. USDI ditto. 11 pp.

1963l   Remarks: Conference on Indian Leadership and Community Development, University of Wisconsin, Eau Claire. USDI ditto. 3 pp.

1963m   Statement: U.S. House of Representatives Subcommittee of the Committee on Interior and Insular Affairs, hearing testimony on HR 1794, HR 3343, and HR 7354, relating to the Allegheny River (Kinzua Dam) Project. USDI litho. 12 pp.

1963n   Address: Unfinished Business—Indian Affairs Today. 20th Annual Convention of the National Congress of American Indians, Bismarck, ND, unpublished MS. 17 pp.

1963o   Address: The New Trail in Indian Affairs. Rocky Mountain College Placement Association, Denver. USDI litho. 24 pp.

1963p   Remarks: Opening a Joint Conference of Canadian and U.S. Administrators of Indian Affairs, Scottsdale, AZ. USDI ditto. 3 pp.

1963q   Remarks: Ground-breaking ceremony for the Burnell Electronics Plant, Laguna, NM. USDI ditto. 2 pp.

1963r   Remarks: Equal Employment Opportunity in the Bureau of Indian Affairs. Equal Employment Opportunity Conference of the Department of Interior, Washington, D.C. 3 pp.

1963s   Address: Adoption of Indian Children. Child Welfare League of America, New York. USDI litho. 18 pp.

1963t   Address: The New Trail in Alaska. Annual Meeting of the Native Brotherhood and Native Sisterhood, Wrangell, AK, unpublished MS. 16 pp.

1964a   Address: The War Against Poverty—The American Indians. Abraham Lincoln Centre, Chicago. USDI litho. 10 pp. Also U.S. GPO 727-429, 8 pp.

1964b   Remarks: City Club of Cleveland. USDI litho. 11 pp.

1964c   Remarks: Fund-raising dinner for American Indian Center, Chicago. 16 pp.

1964d   Remarks: American Indian Capital Conference on Poverty, Washington, D.C. USDI litho. 7 pp.

1964e   Commencement Address: Institute of American Indian Art, Santa Fe. USDI litho. 6 pp.

1964f   Remarks: Golden State Roundup and American Indian Pageant, Oakland, CA. USDI ditto. 2 pp.

1964g   Commencement Address: Laguna-Acoma School, Laguna, NM. USDI ditto. 7 pp.

1964h   Remarks: Adoption ceremony, Minnesota Chippewa tribe, Red Lake, MN, unpublished MS. 12 pp.

1964i   Remarks: Kiwanis Club of Downtown Chicago, unpublished MS. 1 p.

1964j   Remarks: Dedication of Nez Perce Tribal Community Building, Lapwai, ID. USDI litho. 2 pp.

1964k   Remarks: Dedication of Chippewayan Authentics, Inc., Plant, Turtle Mountain Reservation, Belcourt, ND. USDI litho. 2 pp.

1964l   Remarks: Indian Law Committee, Federal Bar Association, Washington, D.C. unpublished MS. 9 pp.

1964m   Address: Seneca Nation, Allegany Reservation, Salamanca, NY, unpublished MS. 5 pp.

1964n   Address: Implementation of the Economic Opportunity Act of 1964. Wisconsin State AFL-CIO Conference, Green Bay, unpublished MS. 6 pp.

1964o   Remarks: Will Rogers Memorial Celebration, Claremore, OK. USDI litho. 4 pp.

1964p   Remarks: Governors' Interstate Indian Council, Denver, CO. USDI litho. 2 pp.

1965a   Statement: U.S. House of Representatives Subcommittee on Indian Affairs of the Committee on Interior and Insular Affairs, Washington, D.C. Committee Print, pp. 76–116.

1965b   Address: Conference on Teaching English to Speakers of Other Languages, San Diego, CA, published MS. 2 pp.

1965c   Remarks: Flag Day ceremonies, Globe, AZ, unpublished MS. 7 pp.

1965d   Address: Education—The Chance to Choose. Fort Lewis College, Durango, CO. U.S. GPO 890-019. 7 pp.

1965e   Address: American Indians and the American Society. Institute on Human Relations, Fisk University, Nashville, TN. U.S. GPO 898-570. 6 pp.

1965f   Remarks: dedication of Neah Bay Job Corps Center, Neah Bay, WA, unpublished MS. 7 pp.

1965g   Remarks: dedication of Stidham Hall, Haskell Institute, Lawrence, KS, unpublished MS. 10 pp.

1965h   Remarks: 21st Annual Convention, National Congress of American Indians, Scottsdale, AZ, unpublished MS. 20 pp.

1966a   Remarks: Symposium on Indian Affairs, Beloit College, Beloit, WI, unpublished MS. 9 pp.

1966b   Lectures: Dillon Lectures on Law and Government, University of South Dakota, Vermillion, transcriptions of audiotapes, unpublished MS.

1966c   Keynote Address: Symposium on American Indians, Oberlin College, Oberlin, OH, unpublished MS. 19 pp.

1969   Paper: Hacia una Definicion de la Cultura de las Reservaciones Indigenas de los Estados Unidos, Annual Meeting of the Society for Applied Anthropology, Mexico City, unpublished MS. 17 pp.

1973a   Statement: before the U.S. House of Representatives Subcommittee on Indian Affairs, in support of the Menominee Restoration Act, Committee Print.

1973b   Commencement Address: After Wounded Knee, What?, University of Wisconsin, Green Bay, unpublished MS.

1973c   Statement: before the U.S. Senate Subcommittee on Indian Affairs, in support of Menominee restoration, unpublished MS. 9 pp.

Miscellaneous

1974   Lecture: Future Anthropology, University of Wisconsin, Milwaukee, unpublished MS. 7 pp.

1979   Remarks: Margaret Mead Memorial Service, American Museum of Natural History, New York, unpublished MS. 3 pp.

1982a   Panelist: Education for Civic Literary and Civic Responsibility, the 1982 Meiklejohn Convocation, University of Wisconsin, Madison, unpublished MS. 3 pp.

1982b   Address: Close to Truman. Annual Business Meeting of the Wisconsin State Historical Society, Wisconsin Rapids, unpublished MS. 3 pp.

1984a   Memorandum: President Truman and Civil Rights, prepared for Truman Centennial Committee, Clark M. Clifford, Chairman, unpublished MS. 8 pp.

1984b   Lecture: The Anthropology of Public Policy, (tape recording), Distinguished Lecture Series, University of Vermont, Burlington.

1986   Interview: Wisconsin Democratic Party Oral History Project, State Historical Society of Wisconsin, Madison (audiotape).

To the reader:

Please fill out this form or a copy and give it to your librarian or information center manager.

Dear _____ :

I recommend for purchase ___ copy(ies) of *Applied Anthropologist and Public Servant: The Life and Work of Philleo Nash* (NAPA Bulletin 7), 1989, Ruth H. Landman and Katherine Spencer Halpern, eds., $7.50, available from:

National Association for the Practice of Anthropology
American Anthropological Association
1703 New Hampshire Avenue, NW
Washington, DC 20009

Sincerely,

_____

(Date) _____   (Title) _____